What can I say about
red-head-Kathy?

Terri J. Zinkel
2014

REDHEADED STEPCHILD

By Terri Jeanne Tinkel

Also by Terri Jeanne Tinkel

OATMEAL AND KISSES

LOVE COMES IN A WHISPER

*****

This is a work of fiction. Names, characters, places and incidents either are the product of the author's imagination or are used fictitiously. Any resemblance to actual persons, living or dead, events, or locales are entirely coincidental.

All rights are reserved. No part of this book may be reproduced in any form or by any means without prior written permission of the author excepting brief quotes used in reviews.

Copywrite ©
By Terri Jeanne Tinkel

In memory of my dear husband

I love you and miss you.

Married 48-½ years

COVER PHOTO: Thank you to my aunt, Kathy Schaff, as the red-headed girl in this photo. I am the small child.

RED HEADED STEP CHILD

By Terri Jeanne Tinkel

RED HEADED STEP CHILD

Historically this expression meant a person who is neglected, mistreated and unwanted. When a red headed child is born to a family of different coloring hair, eyes, skin there is usually a question of the morality of the mother. Sometimes the child suffers abuse or neglect by the other parent.

A red headed child was often distrusted and disliked or thought to be undisciplined.

A red headed stepchild had two counts against it being accepted by the family.

*****

1944 ~

She could smell the cinnamon spice in the hot tea as she held the old china cup in her hands. It was so pleasant to sit quietly and daydream. She was aware of the sound of the crackling logs in the fireplace and the warmth of the fire. She closed her eyes to relax as she felt herself drifting away into sleep.

Her cat, Chloe, snuggled closer on her lap. She automatically stroked Chloe's soft fur and let her mind wander into a happy and familiar daydream. She thought about her husband who had been gone for so long. She hoped there would be a letter today. It had been several weeks since she last heard from him. She knew approximately where he was but, of course, he couldn't or wouldn't tell her. because of regulations. They had only had a few weeks together before he was shipped out to somewhere in Germany. War was tough on him and on her as well.

She started making a list in her head of things she wanted to do when Hank returned home on his next leave. She wasn't used to living on a military base and she hoped she had learned to cook and keep house as well as his mother and her own mother had done.

She had copies of both mothers' favorite recipes and she had been practicing. It wasn't as much fun to cook for only one but at least she had enough left over for meals for a few days at a time.

As the logs burned and shifted in the fireplace, she became aware of a brightness from the window. She opened her eyes slowly and saw snowflakes coming down rapidly. No wonder it was so quiet. Everyone must be inside trying to stay warm and dry. She closed her eyes again and went drifted into sleep again. Chloe was purring and warm, the fire felt so good and she had a stew simmering on the stove. It would taste delicious later when she was ready to eat her supper.

Then she thought she heard something. She opened her eyes and tried to focus. Yes, there it was again! It sounded like someone was shoveling her walkway.

She put Chloe on the floor and tried to get out of the rocking chair. As she struggled to get up, she heard a knock on the door. Who could it be? The snow was coming down very hard and most people would be out of the weather by now. The knock came again, much louder this time. She finally managed to get out of the rocking chair and smoothed her hair and her apron down. She walked to the door and unlocked it.

When she looked out, she couldn't believe her eyes. There was a man all covered in snow, with ice crusted on his hair and his eyelashes. His face was very red as if he had been outside for a long time. He had a scarf wrapped around his face so all she could see were his eyes. She looked behind him and saw that the sidewalk was shoveled and so were the front steps. She cautiously opened the door. She started to say Thank you when the man spoke.

"Honey, don't you recognize me? It's me...Hank! I got a chance to come home for a few days. I guess the telegram I sent didn't arrive because of the snowstorm. They are predicting a blizzard! I sure hope you have enough food for us during the storm. I'll bring in some logs for the fire right now. Well, can't you say anything?"

Nellie Mae just started at him with her mouth open. It couldn't be Hank. He was in Germany, wasn't he? What was he doing here now? Oh dear, what was he going to think of her when he came inside their house? How will she ever explain to him what has been going on?

Nellie Mae sputtered "Hello... I don't know what to say. I'm just so surprised to see you here! I guess I had fallen asleep in front of the fire and I am having trouble getting my thoughts together."

"Um, yes why don't you get some more fire wood for the porch and bring some inside. If there is a blizzard, we will want plenty of dry wood to stay warm. I do have some quilts but it gets cold in the bedroom at night."

"I have a beef stew simmering on the stove and I will make some hot coffee. Or, would you rather have hot tea? I have some good cinnamon spice tea that I like. Oh, I guess I'd better get busy in the kitchen." Nellie Mae quickly shut the door and hurried to the kitchen. "Oh my, what am I going to do?" she said to herself.

Hank walked down the steps and went to the log pile which was covered with an old tarp. He started carrying wood to the porch and then brought some of it into the house. Nellie Mae was busy in the kitchen so he put some logs on the fire and then called out to her.

"Honey, what are you doing? You don't have to fuss with supper yet. Please come here so I can put my arms around you and kiss you. I've missed you so much. Please...please just come here to me."

Nellie Mae smoothed down her dress and apron again and slowly turned to Hank. She walked with her eyes downcast as she approached her husband. Oh, what was he going to say when he realized why she had been avoiding him and his touch. "Oh Lord, please help us now. Please."

As she got closer to Hank, she smiled faintly and told him that she had missed him too and how much she loved him. She placed her soft warm hands on his cold, red face and looked him in the eyes for a long moment. Then she said "I have a lot of things to tell you. I hope you will allow me to say it all and explain."

Nellie Mae took a deep breath and continued "What you might think of me is worrying me. Please, Hank, if you have ever loved me, please let me tell you what has gone on since you've been gone. Will you let me talk without interruption? Will you?"

Hank stared at her with a quizzical look. What in the world was she talking about? Why did Nellie Mae look so frightened? Did she spend all the money he had been sending home? Was she behind in the bills? What was wrong?

Hank smiled at Nellie Mae and said "You can tell me anything. I love you. I don't understand why you are so worried. If you got into financial trouble or had a fight with my mother, it will be just fine. Just sit down by me and tell me what is going on."

Nellie Mae went over to her rocking chair and pulled a quilt over her lap. Then she spoke. "Hank, while you were gone, I saved most of the money you sent home. In fact, I saved quite a bit of it. And I've been learning to cook and keep house too. You know that when I lived at home with Mama, I took care of all my brothers and sisters. Mama did all the housework and the cooking so I never did get much chance to learn her skills. But Bernie had been teaching me. We usually cooked together 2 or 3 days a week and shareed our ration stamps too. It worked out really well for both of us."

Hank interrupted. "That's great, Nellie Mae. The beef stew smells delicious so I guess you HAVE learned to cook. I'm glad because I am very hungry. When I am away in Europe, we don't get a lot of hot meals. And sometimes we don't get to eat often either. But I am sure your cooking will fatten me up in no time at all!" he said with a grin.

"Hank, please let me finish." Nellie Mae begged. "I have a lot of things to tell you and explain to you. It isn't going to be easy and I am afraid that you won't believe me." Nellie Mae' voice broke and she started to cry. "Oh, how am I ever going to make you understand what I did and why I did it?" She buried her face in her hands and cried even harder.

Hank started to get upset. I know it's been hard on you, especially the last several months but just what in the world are you trying to say? Just say it…, Please."

Hank got up from the couch and walked over to Nellie Mae. "Come here and let me put my arms around you. It is going to be ok. Come here, Nellie Mae."

Hank started to remove the quilt from her lap and he pulled her up out of the chair. He put his arms around her and was just beginning to hug her when he felt something. What was that? What was going on?

Hank looked down at Nellie Mae. Tears were running down her face. "What is wrong, Honey? Why are you crying? I'm right here and I am fine. Please tell me."

Nellie Mae looked up at him and brushed the tears from her eyes. Then she took his hand and placed it on the waistband of the apron she was wearing.

"I'm getting to it but it's so hard to tell you. Do you feel that?" she said. Hank looked down and as his hand settled on her apron, he froze.

"What the hell is that?" He demanded. "What have you done? I may not know very much but I know I have been gone for a year and it takes 9 months to have a baby! Whose child is it? And why did you cheat on me? I was fighting for our country in a horrible war and you did this? All that has kept me going was thinking of you waiting back here for me so we could spend the rest of our lives together! How could you betray me like that?" Hank grabbed his coat and started for the door.

Nellie Mae cried out. "Hank, Hank, wait! I can explain. It's not what you think. I didn't cheat on you at all. I can explain everything, Please, let me tell you what happened!"

Hank stopped and his face went white. "Did someone do this to you? Did some jerk force himself on you because I was gone? Who was he? Where is he? I'll find him and Ill make him wish he had never ...What's been going on here?"
\
Nellie Mae took a deep breath and then she asked Hank to sit down on the couch with her while she told him why she was so upset.

Hank sat down heavily into the seat. "I'm ready to listen. I'm not sure about this but I will listen. I told you that I would ~ so it had better be good.!"

Nellie Mae took another breath and started to explain.....

CHAPTER ONE ~

Nellie Mae had grown up as the oldest child in a family of 5 other brothers and sisters. Her father worked very hard to provide for the family. Times were tough back in the 30's. It was lucky that her mother, Mary, was so good at making food stretch. She could make a tasty meal out of a few scraps of meat and lots of carrots. beans and potatoes. She also was an excellent baker and her homemade bread was the first thing that everyone grabbed at the table.

In addition, her mother also had a lot of sewing skills and often made clothes for the children out of hand-me-downs, her old dresses or her husband's old work shirts and pants. She got feed sacks from a farmer who came to town to sell his eggs and chickens. She could usually pick out some lovely patterned feed sacks and make some very nice and unique clothing for the children.

Because she had so many children and so many chores, she expected Nellie Mae to take care of the smaller children and keep them occupied so Mary could sew for hours without interruption.

Nellie Mae would make up stories. She read the children lots of books and she made up games for them to play too. But Nellie Mae never had a chance to learn her mother's skills of sewing and cooking and housekeeping.

Nellie Mae lived in a small town near Chicago with her family and loved the neighborhood. She had grown up with her grandparents living close by too. She spent most of her time with her family.

She also had some girlfriends and they often went to the movies or the library or the little diner just a block or two away. It was a quiet life but Nellie Mae was content. She expected that some day she would marry and have children of her own. She hoped she would eventually learn to cook and clean because she would have to be able to take care of her own family. She didn't know how many children she wanted. Having 5 brothers and sisters was a lot and she didn't think she wanted a family as large as her parents had.

After high school, she took a couple of classes at the local college. She also found a job working in a candy store about 2 blocks from her house. She loved to walk into the shop and get the first whiff of the chocolates. **"It is just like Heaven would smell."** thought Nellie Mae.

When talk turned to a war starting over in Germany and Poland, many of her girlfriends wanted to do something to help the soldiers. None of them were very skilled at knitting. They tried rolling bandages but that was a bit boring. They helped collect metal cans and learned how to do without stockings. Meatless meals at home became more than a once a week occurrence.

One day all the girlfriends met at the diner. One of the friends, by the name of Bernadette, came in all excited. "I just heard there is going to be a Red Cross Canteen starting next month! Isn't that the best news ever?"

Nellie Mae asked. "Bernie, what's a Canteen? And why are you so excited about it? Sit down and tell us what you know about the details!"

Bernie told them what she had heard about it. "There's going to be punch and cookies, coffee or tea. Maybe even Coca Cola on occasion! There will be records for dancing. And sometimes, there might be a live band or a well-known singer!"

"But better than that...can you imagine how many good looking soldiers or sailors might be there? We can dance all evening and be chaperoned by the Red Cross volunteers. So our parents should not have any problem letting us go! Let's go sign up right now!"

One of the girls wondered if they should discuss it with their parents first. But the other girls decided it would be more responsible to find out details before they figured out how to approach their parents for permission. If they had good answers for all the questions, how could their parents object?

All the girlfriends went down to the Red Cross and talked to the volunteers about the Canteen. It really sounded great. They could have a good time even with being chaperoned and meet some **real men**. On the way home, all the girls talked about what they would wear and how they should do their hair. They could hardly wait for the first Canteen to be held.

CHAPTER TWO ~

Several weeks later, Nellie Mae had been going to the Canteen dances almost every weekend. She hadn't met any man who really interested her. Most of them were just there for the free food and the dancing. Many of them couldn't dance well. Some of them couldn't even carry on a conversation!

The Red Cross volunteers were good chaperons too. If they saw any one who seemed to be getting out of line with the girls, the men were immediately escorted to the door and put on a list and not allowed back in again. Some of the men had even tried to sneak alcohol into the Canteen and were thrown out. Nellie Mae kept going because her girlfriends wanted to go. And she enjoyed the dancing too.

On December 7, 1941, the world changed for all the girls and their parents. Pearl Harbor was attacked by Japan. Everyone was fearful that the war might come to the United States. It was unimaginable to think they might not be safe in their own country.

Many of the local boys were anxious to sign up in spite of the fear of their family members. The war efforts were intensified and everyone was trying to do all they could to support the military, especially the men and women in all the services that they had come to know at the Canteen.

Finally, near the end of the year, Nellie Mae and her friends heard there would be a huge fancy New Year's Eve Dance. Everyone was to bring donations of food or clothing or anything that could be used in the war effort.

But it would still be a big party too. They would be wearing their best dresses. The military were required to wear their dress uniforms this time.. There was a rumor that a real band might be coming to play. Maybe it would be Tommy Dorsey with his new male singer, Frank Sinatra! What a thrill it would be to see those blue eyes and hear Frankie singing all those great love songs like **_I'll Never Smile Again_** and **_I'll Be Seeing You_**. All the girls could talk about nothing else but the New Year's Eve dance.

Nellie Mae's mother told her daughter that she would make her a one-of-a-kind dress out of some lace curtain material she had saved. Her mother was really excited to work on something so beautiful for her oldest daughter. It was much more satisfying, challenging and rewarding than sewing shirts and pants and simple dresses for the children, especially for the boys who always had torn clothing to mend.

When the big night finally arrived, all the girls met at Nellie Mae's house and got dressed together. They did each other's hair and makeup and chattered as they put on their special dresses for the evening. Each and every one of them wore a different color dress and they looked like a rainbow of lovely flowers when they were all ready to go. They reluctantly put on their old winter coats over their beautiful outfits and set off walking to the Canteen.

When they arrived, they could hardly believe the change in the room. It was decked out in all sorts of special décor. Beautiful tablecloths were spread on the tables. There were several different kinds of cookies and cakes and pies. There were snacks, cheese and crackers, little sandwiches and celery sticks filled with peanut butter or cream cheese. There was punch and coffee, lemonade and soda too. It was like a banquet.

And the girls, who were in attendance, were all dressed in their best gowns. Colors of every imaginable hue were swirling all over the dance floor. And the military men...**oh the men...**were dressed in their uniforms with their ribbons and medals all displayed. Their boots were shined and they looked magnificent.

Nellie Mae and her friends were almost speechless. How in the world would they ever get through this evening without falling in love? It was inevitable that at least one of them would meet the man of her dreams. Who would it be?"

The girls all agreed that this could be the beginning of a wonderful new year. Each of them was nervous to see if they would fill up their dance cards and dance with someone very special.

They eagerly smiled at the passing parade of men and hoped to be picked for the first dance of the evening. It wasn't long before their little pastel programs were filled with the names of the men who would claim them for every dance.

CHAPTER THREE ~

Bernie floated by in a lovely dress of pale green. It went so well with her strawberry blond hair. Her green eyes were sparkling like emeralds. She hummed along with the music. She looked like an angel in Paradise. The other girls were equally as pretty in their dresses too. Most of them had a dance partner and were enjoying the beautiful fox trot and other slow dances. It looks like a room full of flowers just drifting along on a soft summer breeze.

Nellie Mae was sitting by herself at the side of the room. Her dress was stunning. But she felt awkward in such a grown-up gown. Her dark hair was piled up in a chignon with a white flower made out of the same lace as her dress. Her blue eyes were wide open just watching everything that was going on. Her friend, Bernie, had even squirted a tiny bit of her own perfume on Nellie Mae. It was called Evening In Paris and it came in a beautiful cobalt blue bottle with a tiny tassel on the cap.

As Nellie Mae watched her friends dance around the room, she noticed that a man was approaching her. She hoped he was just going to sit down in a chair near her. She still wasn't used to talking to men. She was more used to talking to her brothers who were just boys ...*noisy and dirty boys at that.*

The man pulled over one of the chairs and sat beside her. He cleared his throat and then he introduced himself. "Hello, my name is Harold Hamilton. I've been in the Army for about a year now. I've seen you here at the other Canteen dances before. But I have never seen you dressed up in such a lovely gown. It reminds me of my mother's favorite lace tablecloth."

"Oh my, I wasn't being disrespectful or saying that your gown looks like a tablecloth! I hope that you were not insulted by my careless remark." Hank said nervously.

Nellie Mae smiled. "Oh no, actually my mother made it for me out of some lace curtains she saved. And it is probably the most beautiful gown I've ever had. She made it especially for this dance tonight. I'm glad you like it."

"My nickname is Hank. So, um...so what's your name?" Hank said with a smile.

"Oh, my name is Nellie Mae Hill. I live at home with my parents and my five brothers and sisters. I work at a candy store two blocks from home and I...oh wait. you probably don't want to know my life history." Nellie Mae stopped and then looked down at her lap. She wrung her hands with a tiny hankie her mother had made for her. She could feel how hot her cheeks were so she knew she was probably blushing too.

"I'm glad to meet you, Nellie Mae. That's an unusual name. Are you named after someone in your family?" Hank asked.

Nellie Mae responded. "Well, yes I am. My grandmother's name is Nell and my mother's name is Mary so it's a combination of both, I guess. I like it too. It's unusual and it seems to suit me very well."

Hank smiled and said "Yes, it does. I do like it. It's not only unusual but very special too since you are named after two women in your family. So you have a lot of brothers and sisters~! I am an only child. My parents weren't too happy that I joined up so quickly when the rumors of a war started but I felt like I had to do my duty for our country."

"So, now that we have introduced ourselves to each other, may I have the next dance, Nellie Mae? I promise not to step on your toes if I can help it. What do you say?"

Nellie Mae blushed again and said "Yes, you may. I'm not the best dancer but I think I can handle a slow dance if you promise not to laugh."

"Oh, I won't laugh, not at all!" Hank said with a smile. You should have seen me when my mother taught me. At least I shouldn't step on your toes."

The next dance started and it was a lovely waltz. Hank reached out for Nellie Mae's hand and pulled her up out of her chair. He led her to the dance floor and put his hand out to take hers and they began to dance to the music.

It seemed like a dream to Nellie Mae. This handsome soldier was waltzing her around the dance floor. It felt like they were gliding on ice and every note of the music was glorious. Was this what falling in love felt like? Nellie Mae thought. If it was, then she liked it. She liked it very much.

She closed her eyes and just listened to the music and followed Hank's lead. When the band stopped playing, she opened her eyes and saw her best friend, Bernie near her. Bernie had a big grin on her face and winked at Nellie Mae.

Bernie gave her a hug and asked if she wanted to freshen up in the ladies room. As they walked away from the dance floor, Hank said he would get them some punch and be waiting near the chairs where they had been sitting earlier. Nellie Mae just smiled and grabbed Bernie's arm. She leaned in and whispered "Oh, Bernie, isn't he the most handsome man you have ever seen?"

Bernie laughed and said "Have you looked at MY partner? His name is Edison Dawson. He calls himself Ed. He is also in the Army and he knows Hank Hamilton too. They are serving in the same unit. They are here for additional training before they have to ship out for somewhere overseas. I think I am in love! Or at the very least, I like him quite a bit."

Bernie continued. "Why don't you spend the night with me and we can talk about our men. There's so much I have to tell you. Both of them seem so nice, so respectful and so courageous to be shipping out to fight for our country in this war!"

Nellie Mae agreed to spend the night. She also wanted to talk about the men and her feelings and what in the world had happened in such a short time. One dance and she felt like she was walking on air. Was this normal? Or was she just living a fantasy? Was it possible to fall in love with someone so quickly? Was this just infatuation or could it possibly be real? Things like this didn't happen to her. She was a small town girl and maybe she was just jumping to conclusions.

After a quick trip to the restroom to check their makeup in the mirror, the girls returned to the chairs at the side of the room. Ed had walked over and was waiting with Hank for the return of their dance partners. The men explained that they would be shipping out eventually but first they had to continue with more training. They would be in the area for a few months until their unit was called up.

When the dance was over, the men asked if they could walk the girls home.

"Of course", both Bernie and Nellie Mae said. Nellie Mae explained she needed to stop at her home first to ask her parents if she could spend the night with Bernie. She also wanted to introduce Hank to her parents so she could ask them what they thought of him later. Her parent's impression of Hank would be important to Nellie Mae if this relationship was going to go anywhere.

The two couples set out to walk the girls home. They did stop at Nellie Mae's house and were introduced to her parents. Nellie Mae got permission to spend the night with Bernie. Then the two couples walked a few more blocks to the diner and had some hot cocoa. After some more discussion, the girls said they needed to go to Bernie's house. So the men accompanied the girls to Bernie's and met her parents too. Then the men asked for the girls phone numbers and left.

The girls were so excited to talk about the evening that they excused themselves and went straight up to Bernie's bedroom. As they changed out of their gowns, they started chattering as quickly as they could to discuss each and every remark the men had made during the evening.

They each agreed that both of the men were great. They were very impressed with the men's manners. And both girls wondered if the men would call them later in the week.

CHAPTER FOUR ~

The men did call the girls before the end of the week. They invited them to the movies on Saturday when they would have a 12 hour pass. They went to see **HIS GIRL FRIDAY** with Cary Grant and took the girls to the diner for dessert and hot cocoa. The evening went by very quickly. They all had a good time talking and getting to know each other even better.

Every time the men had a chance, they contacted the girls and went on double dates. They also went together to the Canteen dances as often as they could. By now, both the girls thought they had found their *Prince Charmings*. They spend many nights talking about the relationships and wondering where it would lead. They realized the men were going to be shipped out eventually. They wanted to spend as much time with them as they could.

The parents felt much better when the two couples went everywhere together. They didn't want anything to happen if each couple was alone too often. The young men seemed very nice and were attentive to the girls as well as very respectful to the girls' parents.

After about 2 months, Hank and Ed took the girls out for dinner. They told them both that the rumor was that they would be shipping out in about 6 weeks. Of course, the girls were devastated. What would they do without Hank and Ed around?

Both girls told the men that they would write every day and do whatever they could to support the war effort.

Hank and Ed had each decided they were going to walk their own girl home and have a serious talk with their date. Ed and Hank felt strongly that they wanted a permanent understanding with their girls. They wanted the girls to always be in their lives. As they said their goodbyes that night, Hank and Ed each asked their girl to walk home separately.

Ed and Bernie started out for her home. Ed wanted to see if Bernie was committed to a relationship with him. If she was, he intended to ask her father for permission to marry Bernie before he shipped out. As they talked about their future and their hopes and dreams, it became evident that Bernie was in love with Ed. She promised to wait for him until he came back from the war. She told him that she loved him with all her heart and wanted nothing more than to be with him forever.

As they parted that night, Ed knew he would be having that talk with Bernie's father shortly. He didn't want to wait until he came back from the war. He wanted a wife and to start a family as soon as possible.

Hank and Nellie Mae had a similar conversation. Hank told her that he knew she was very close to her family. He asked her if she thought she could leave her home and live somewhere else some day. She said she was sure that she could but she wondered where that would be and when.

Hank said if he got promoted, he could qualify for a unit on a base somewhere. He didn't know where yet but he intended to talk to his Chaplain when he got back to the base in town. He asked Nellie Mae if she would honor him by marrying him some day. Nellie Mae smiled and said "Of course, I love you, Hank."

When Nellie Mae went inside her house, her mother was waiting up for her. Mary asked her daughter why she was smiling and had such a glow. Nellie

Mae explained about the serious conversation she had just had with Hank. She told her mother what his intentions were and that she thought she might be informally engaged.

Mary smiled and said "Hank's a fine man. I know he loves you. I also know he will take good care of you. But remember, he is going off to war. He might not come back very soon. He might come back wounded or he might not come back at all. It's a serious decision to make. Maybe it would be better if you waited for him to see how you both feel in a year or so. Just think about it, dear."

Nellie Mae went to bed and thought about the entire evening. Then she thought about the short time she had known Hank. Was this REALLY love? Was she just in love with the idea of being married and becoming a wife and even a mother? Was she ready to leave her home and her family? Could she be happy living on a base alone without Hank for months at a time?

What about her girlfriends? What about Bernie? Did Ed and Bernie also have a conversation about their futures tonight? She couldn't wait to talk to

Bernie in the morning. She wanted to compare notes with her and find out what Bernie thought about this whole idea.

Maybe they could live on the same base together if both couples got married! That wouldn't be so bad. Bernie was a great cook and she could teach Nellie Mae how to be a good housekeeper.

CHAPTER FIVE ~

The next few days went by in a blur. Nellie Mae and Bernie had a lot of long serious discussions. They daydreamed about being married and having children. They fantasized about living on the same base and sharing their skills and recipes and spending as much time together as possible while their men ~ their HUSBANDS ~ were away. Could it really work out for them? Were both girls really ready to commit to a marriage when they were so young?

The following Saturday night, both men had called their girls and made a date. They took the girls out for dinner again and then said they each wanted some time alone with their girl. As the two couples separated for the evening, Nellie Mae and Bernie hugged each other and Bernie whispered "Call me in the morning or come over so we can talk."

Bernie and Ed started walked towards her home. When they got there, Ed asked to come inside for a moment to say hello to her parents. As they opened the door, the room was filled with her family. They were smiling. There was a cake on the dining room table and everyone was looking excited.

Bernie turned to see what Ed's reaction was. He was down on one knee with a small ring box in his hand. He said " I love you, Bernadette. I've asked your father for permission to have your hand in marriage. He has agreed…so if you'll have me, I want to ask you to be my wife. I love you and I don't want to wait until I come home from the war. I want to get married right away. Will you marry me, my darling Bernadette? Will you please be my wife?"

Bernie turned to look at her parents. They were both smiling and nodded that they were giving their permission. Bernie turned back to Ed and said "Oh yes, I love you too, Ed. I want to be your wife forever and ever. I want to get married as soon as we can make arrangements. Please, let's do it right away!"

With that, the room was filled with laughter and hugs and smiling. Everyone was congratulating everyone and talking at once. Everyone had an opinion of when and where the marriage should take place and where Bernie would live while Ed was overseas. They all agreed that until Bernie could move to a base, she would continue to live at home with her parents for the time being.

Finally, Ed pulled Bernie aside and said "I've talked to the Base Chaplain. He can marry us as soon as we get the license and blood tests. We can be married in just a few days if that is what you want."

Ed continued "If you want a fancy wedding, it will take longer and I may not have the time. Think about it over night and talk to Nellie Mae because I know both you girls share everything. You can let me know when you have decided what you want. I love you so much, Bernie, and I can't wait to be your husband!"

Bernie agreed to think seriously about it. She wanted to talk to her parents and to Nellie Mae too. Maybe Nellie Mae got a proposal tonight as well. Maybe they could have a double wedding ceremony! There were plenty of decisions to be made in such a short time.

She did like the idea of the Base Chaplain performing the ceremony. Ed could wear his dress uniform and she could wear …she could wear …*something*. So she kissed Ed good night and closed the door.

She decided to go straight to bed and start thinking of what she wanted to do. In the morning, she would talk to her parents and to Nellie Mae, of course. Then she would have a better idea of what plans she needed to make and how soon this could all take place.

CHAPTER SIX ~

The next morning, Bernie got up early and walked to Nellie Mae's house. She knocked at the door. Nellie Mae opened the front door and smiled. "So, do you have anything new to tell me today, Bernie?"

They both giggled and hugged and started talking at once. Bernie told Nellie Mae what had gone on at her house the night before. Then Bernie asked, "OK, Nellie Mae, what happened with you last night? Do YOU have anything to tell me?"

Nellie Mae got tears in her eyes. "Oh, Bernie, it was so romantic. Hank came in and asked my parents for my hand in marriage right in front of them and all my brothers and sisters. He said he loved me with all his heart and wanted me to marry him. He said if I agreed, he would take me to a jeweler today and get me an engagement ring. He said he wanted us to spend our lives together forever. And he wants to get married now and not wait until after the war is over. And he said..."

"So, what did you say, Nellie Mae? Did you accept his proposal?" Bernie interrupted. "Tell me right this instant, I can't wait to hear the answer!"

"Well, of course, I said yes!" Nellie Mae responded. "I will be talking to my parents later this morning about my thoughts and plans. I want to have a small wedding here at home. I want to wear the white lace dress my mother made for me for the New Year's Eve dance. She can probably make a veil too. I want all my family and friends to be here too. This is the most romantic thing that has ever happened to me. I feel so lucky to have found Hank."

Nellie Mae continued. "What about you and Ed, Bernie? Did he ask you to marry him too? And if he did, did you say Yes? You did, didn't you? Tell me that you did!" Nellie Mae said with a smile.

Bernie laughed. "Of course, I did! Here's my engagement ring to prove it! I love Ed so much. He wants us to get married by the Base Chaplain on base. Would you consider a double wedding ceremony? It would be so great to get married together"

"Bernie. I don't think that's the right idea. I want both of our weddings to be special for each of us. Besides, then we can be maids of honor for each other or Matron of Honor depending on which of us gets married first. Would that be okay with you?"

Bernie smiled. "Of course, it is just fine with me. You're right. We should each have our own special day. We will enjoy both weddings that way."

"So, what do you think I should wear to my wedding? Should I get a new dress or a suit? Should I wear a hat and carry a bouquet too?" Bernie questioned.

Nellie Mae grinned. "We have a lot of plans to make, don't we? I can't wait to tell the rest of our girlfriends too. Won't they be surprised that two of our group got proposed to last night and will be getting married soon...very soon!"

CHAPTER SEVEN ~

Within a few days, both girls and their families and the prospective grooms had plans made and were working on getting everything done as quickly as possible. Bernie and Ed were going to be married first. The Base Chaplain was helping them organize a military wedding with all the pomp and circumstance he could arrange on such short notice. It would be a very special and memorable ceremony. Nellie Mae would be Bernie's maid of honor and Hank would be Ed's best man.

Bernie decided to buy a suit. It would be something to make her feel more grownup and it would be practical too. Nellie Mae took Bernie shopping and they found a suit in a lovely shade of blue-green that set off her strawberry blonde hair and made her eyes look enormous. She practiced with various hair styles and finally decided on a page boy.

When the big day came, she was calm and poised. She got ready with the help of her maid of honor, Nellie Mae. Nellie bought her a blue and silver pin to wear on her suit and a white silk garter. Bernie's mother gave her an old penny to put in her shoe. And Nellie Mae's mother, Mary, loaned her the lace handkerchief that Nellie Mae was going to use in her wedding in a few weeks.

The ceremony was lovely. The weather was perfect and everything went off with no problems. Ed had two days off and was taking Bernie to a small cabin that a friend had loaned to him. He hoped to start their marriage off happily and if Bernie was pregnant by the time he had to ship out, then his life would be perfect.

They left on their short honeymoon and had two wonderful days together. They were alone and spent hours talking and laughing and making love. Bernie even thought she might have gotten pregnant but of course, she really had no idea if she was already.

Besides, Nellie Mae's wedding was coming up in a few weeks so Bernie wanted to be as much a part of that event as possible. She felt very grownup now that she knew what it was like to be a wife. She thought she could answer any questions Nellie Mae might have about what it was like to be married.

The girls had always been very close and Bernie was sure that Nellie Mae might have questions that she would be too embarrassed to ask her mother, Mary. Besides they were young brides married to real military men so things were probably different than when their mothers got married. After all, it was the 1940's!

CHAPTER EIGHT ~

The date for Hank and Nellie Mae's wedding finally arrived. The house had been thoroughly cleaned and everything that could be washed and starched and ironed was taken care of. Mary had been cooking up all sorts of fancy food and working on a trousseau for Nellie Mae.

She had put all of her daughters to work embroidering pillowcases and towels. She had made a tablecloth and napkins with Hank and Nellie Mae's initials on it. She had asked friends and family to help with other items so Nellie Mae would have plenty of things to take with her to remind her of her friends and family back home.

Nellie Mae did wear the lace gown she had worn to the New Year's Eve party. The veil was simple but beautiful and was trimmed with some of the same lace as the dress. Nellie Mae carried the lace hanky that her mother, Mary, had loaned to Bernie.

Bernie loaned her the blue and silver pin to wear and Bernie's mother asked her to wear her own lovely pearl necklace. Mary made her veil so Nellie Mae had something old, something new, something borrowed and something blue at her wedding ceremony too.

Hank was so handsome in his dress uniform. His shoes were shined so brightly they looked like satin. His best man was Ed. The Base Chaplain had agreed to perform the ceremony in Nellie Mae's home as well.

As Nellie Mae's sister played the wedding march on the living room piano, Nellie Mae walked down the stairs in her lovely gown. Everyone gasped at the glow on her face. She looked like an angel. She was so happy, she was almost floating to the front of the fireplace where Hank was waiting. The wedding vows were quickly exchanged. The reception followed in the dining room. Everyone complimented Mary on all the fine food.

Within an hour or so, Hank whispered in Nellie Mae's ear. " Honey, it's time for us to go. We only have two days and I want to spend every second with you alone. Please say your goodbyes to your friends and family so we can get going. I love you so much, my darling."

Nellie Mae hugged and kissed all her family and friends. She whispered to her best friend, Bernie. "I can't believe we are both married ladies now! I can't wait to go on my honeymoon but I also can't wait to come home to talk to you. Have you heard anything more about when our husbands might have to ship out?"

Bernie whispered back. "I haven't heard anything yet but I think it won't be long now. I hope you and Hank have a wonderful time. Stay happy and positive for him. I'm sure he is worried already about leaving you."

Hank and Nellie Mae drove to the next town where he had made a reservation in a hotel for them. They had dinner out, champagne and spent hours in their room with the Do Not Disturb sign on the door. After the two days were over, they returned back to Nellie Mae's home.

Hank told her he had to return to the base. He would be talking to the Commander about when he could get base housing so Nellie Mae could be with him all the time. He promised to call her in the morning.

"I don't want to leave you, my dearest darling girl. But I have to. I know you understand and that you will be supportive as we try to get our living arrangements sorted out. Be brave and always remember that I love you." Hank said to her.

He then spoke to her parents in private and reassured them that he was doing everything in his power to get Nellie Mae to be able to live with him on the base.

CHAPTER NINE~

In a few more weeks, Ed and Hank decided it was time to take their wives out for a dinner and have a talk with them. As they picked up the girls, they each had very serious looks on their faces and they were very solemn.

Both of the girls had been chattering together as they walked to the restaurant but then they realized their husbands were not saying very much. Bernie and Nellie Mae exchanged worried looks. They walked quietly the rest of the way to the restaurant and took their seats. They both folded their hands and waited.

Ed started talking first. "Ok, girls, here's the news. We have to ship out in two weeks. We can't tell you where we are going but we can say it will be a very important mission. We are ready to go because we have worked very hard to prepare. The good thing is we already have our overseas addresses so you can start writing right away. We will both be writing back to you as much as possible."

"The other good thing is we will have a few days leave before we have to go. So, we want to take both of you away on another honeymoon. What do you say?"

Bernie burst into tears. "Oh no. I knew this was coming but I guess I was hoping it never would. Oh, Ed. I love you so much. I am glad we will have a few days together. And Nellie Mae and I will become even closer as Army wives while the two of you are away. I can't imagine not talking to you on a regular basis. But I am a good writer so I will talk to you in my letters."

Hank turned to Nellie Mae. "Another piece of good news is that we found out that we should be able to have base housing very soon. If our mission goes well, we were promised to get our stripes and be promoted. We will be gone by the time the orders come through so you will have to move there by yourselves but hopefully you can get assigned to housing close to each other. And we know your families will help you pack and get settled in"

"I know you both want to be together as much as possible. I also know both of you are very brave and strong and will get through this as well as you can." Hank said as he put his arm around Nellie Mae.

Nellie Mae leaned over and kissed Hank's cheek. "I love you so much, Hank. I will do everything in my power to stay positive and brave for you. And if the housing doesn't come through, I will continue to live with my parents and keep on working at the candy store. I'll save up my money and I'll learn to cook and clean and be a perfect housewife by the time you come home again."

Both men breathed a sigh of relief that their wives had taken the news so well. They knew that the girls were in for some tough times but they also knew the girls would be sticking together and be supportive to each other too. Hank and Ed had already vowed to watch each other's backs and to take care of each other's wives if any happened to one of them.

CHAPTER TEN ~

The two couples decided to go to a small city close by to spend their last few days together. They saw movies and went dancing and ate out at diners. They saw a ballgame and had hot dogs and ice cream as they cheered on the teams. They took photographs and tried to stay as upbeat as possible.

Their nights were spent alone in long hours of love making. They told their spouses their hopes and dreams, their fears and their future plans. They talked about the number of children they wanted to have and what names they would like to give the babies. They laughed and they cried together. It was a beautiful time to share in spite of the worries and concerns they all had.

All too soon, they had to come back home. The girls went back to their parents' homes. The men went back to their base. When the men got the final orders, they were given an 24 hour leave and went immediately to their wives. Both families had arranged for a combined big send-off dinner and talked long into the night.

The next day, the men returned to the base where there were buses ready to take them to their next destination. As the men hugged and kissed their wives and their new extended families, they vowed to return safely to start a new life as married couples.

Ed whispered into Bernie's ear. "Do you think you might be pregnant? I was hoping you might be because I want nothing more than a family to come home to. Please let me know if you are, my darling."

Bernie blushed and said. "Well, I don't know yet but its a good possibility since we spent so much of our time in bed together! And yes, I will let you know as soon as possible. If I am, I will tell you everything about the pregnancy and have Nellie Mae take photographs of me as my tummy gets bigger, OK?"

While Ed and Bernie were whispering quietly, Hank and Nellie Mae were talking too. Hank and Nellie Mae had not wanted to start a family until he returned from the war. But if Nellie Mae was already pregnant, Hank wanted her to know it would be wonderful.

Nellie Mae whispered to Hank. "I don't think I am pregnant and that's just fine with me. I will have plenty to do while you are away. I want to become a good cook and learn how to fix your favorite recipes. Your mother has invited me to visit and she said she will give me the recipes for all your favorite dishes to learn too."

"I love you with all my heart and soul, Hank. I will be writing you every day and praying for you every night. Take good care of yourself and of Ed, too, of course."

Hank hugged Nellie Mae closely to his chest. He said "I love you too, my darling. I will pray to see you again in my dreams every night. If you are pregnant, I will love the baby with all my heart too. Try not to worry about me and take care of yourself and take care of Bernie too."

The men both turned to each other's wives and gave them hugs and kisses too. Then the men moved on to speak with the parents and family of both girls. They promised to write and to be as careful as they could be. And the families told both men that they would be watching out for the girls as well.

Soon it was time to get on the bus. Ed and Hank found a seat together and opened up the window to say goodbye again. The girls waved as the bus left the base. Then, they burst into tears and hugged each other tightly. They vowed to stay strong and to be there for each other every day. As their families gathered around to support the girls, they all decided it was time to go home and start writing letters.

CHAPTER ELEVEN ~

During the next few weeks, Nellie Mae was doing her best to learn to cook and keep house. She had a lot of practice with her mother's assistance. Bernie also helped Nellie Mae learn some of Bernie's own special dishes. They spent every evening together, writing letters to their husbands and talking. They tried to keep the letters upbeat and cheerful and talk about things going on at home.

A few more weeks after the men had left, Bernie came over with a big smile on her face. She grabbed Nellie Mae and pulled her up the stairs to Nellie Mae's bedroom. She quickly closed the bedroom door and told Nellie Mae to sit down.

"What is going on, Bernie?" Nellie Mae asked her friend. "You are very excited and your face is just glowing."

"I'm pregnant! Bernie giggled. "I just went to the doctor to be sure. He said I am about 7 weeks pregnant. I can't wait to write to Ed and tell him. He wanted a family so much and now he will have one. I am so excited!"

"I can't wait to start showing. I want you to take photographs every week of me so I can send them to Ed. You will, won't you?"

"Oh, Nellie Mae, do you think you might be pregnant too? Wouldn't it be wonderful if we were both pregnant and had our babies about the same time?" Bernie said with a giggle.

Nellie Mae quickly said. "I'm not pregnant. Hank and I really didn't plan for it. And it is better right now for us that I am not. I have so many things to learn and to do. Besides I am working at the candy store and I am trying to get more hours so I can save more money. But I am so happy for you and Ed. And of course, I will take photographs of you every week if you want me to."

"So, how are you feeling? I've heard about morning sickness, are you having any? I can't wait to hear what Ed thinks of this. And do you mind if I write and tell Hank too?"

"Let me tell Ed first, please."Bernie said. "But then you can tell Hank. After all, you two will be like the baby's aunt and uncle. Maybe even the baby's godparents if that is possible. And I have more big news."

"What else could be more exciting than this news about the baby?" Nellie Mae said. "So what is it?"

Bernie said with a big grin "The orders for us to move to a base are coming through in the next month or two! The men got promoted while they are over there fighting and therefore, the Army Chaplin contacted me that we can move onto the base. He even is going to try to get us housing next door to each other. Isn't that exciting? Wow, how our lives have changed in the past year! Would you have ever imagined how different 1942 would be for us? And what is 1943 going to bring?" Bernie added. "Besides a baby, of course!" she giggled.

Nellie Mae smiled back. "Well, I don't know what to think. I sure didn't expect that so soon! That is big news!. Bigger than I ever expected to hear so quickly. We have a lot of plans to make and things to pack up. I guess we had better tell our parents so they can help us decide what to do. I know they will help us move and get settled if they can. Will we get orders on what we need to do, do you think?" Nellie asked.

Bernie answered. "The Chaplain said he would have the paperwork sent to us as soon as the housing is assigned. Yes, we have to follow orders just like our men do. Should we tell our husbands about the housing or wait until it is confirmed? What do you think, Nellie Mae?"

"Let's wait, Bernie. That way we will be sure and we will have the new addresses. We can tell them when we are ready to make the move. Now I guess you need to write Ed that special letter about the baby." Nellie Mae added.

"Right, I do. But first I am going to take a little nap on your bed. You don't mind, do you? I am really tired." Bernie said as she yawned and stretched out on the bed.

"Go ahead and sleep, Bernie. You need to rest, I know. I'll go downstairs and see what my mother is up to while you rest. I love you, little mother." Nellie Mae leaned over and tucked a quilt around her friend who had already closed her eyes and fallen asleep.

CHAPTER TWELVE ~

It wasn't long before Ed had written back to Bernie. He was so excited about the baby. He was sure it was going to be a boy and he already was thinking of names. He told Bernie he never thought he could love her more until now. He was so anxious to see photographs and wanted Bernie to tell him everything about the pregnancy. He cautioned her to take it easy and not to overdo. He expressed his joy and love and pride over and over.

In the meantime, Bernie was having a tough time with the pregnancy. The morning sickness had come on with a vengeance. She could hardly eat or get out of bed. The doctor was concerned but assured her that usually the nausea went away after the first 3 months. Bernie forced herself to eat when she could. She consumed a lot of crackers and milk and oatmeal. She was gaining some weight but not a lot. She was exhausted and looked very gaunt. Nellie Mae tried to spend as much time with her as possible. Nellie Mae secretly was glad that she wasn't pregnant too. If this was what it was like, she wasn't sure she wanted to ever be pregnant.

A few weeks later, the wives got paperwork from the base that their housing had been assigned. They were going to live next door to each other just as they had hoped. They got a list of what they could bring, what they had to do to meet the requirements of base living and when they could move in. They talked to their parents and started gathering together all the things they would need. And one weekend, they moved.

The wives were so thrilled to have their own places. It really made them feel like they were adults at last. They were married to soldiers and they felt so proud. The first thing both of them decided to do was to help each other unpack. They unpacked and arranged all of Bernie's things first so if she needed to rest, there was space for her to do so.

Then they decided to take a break at Nellie Mae's unit and write letters to their husbands telling them that they were actually moved in. After they had unpacked at Nellie's new home, they took photographs of both units and promised to sent them with the next letters. They could hardly wait to get their first mail with their new addresses on the envelope.

The girls also agreed to cook together and share their recipes and food so they each wouldn't have to buy as much. They could put their ration stamps together and have some extra sugar and coffee too.

They continued to settle in and found their little units were quite cozy. They loved sharing the letters they each received from their husbands. They talked about everything under the sun including Bernie's ongoing pregnancy and Nellie Mae's efforts to find another job since she was too far away from her home town to work at the candy store.

Bernie was starting to feel a bit better and she was putting on some weight. Her pregnancy was starting to show just a little. Of course, she was constantly pulling down on her dress to make the rounded bump show up more too. She was so proud to be pregnant with her first child.

Bernie was constantly telling Nellie Mae about things the other military wives had told her about pregnancy and child birth and raising an infant. She wanted to be the most informed and best new mother ever.

Bernie made an appointment with the base doctor to care for her during the pregnancy. She wanted to do everything in her power to make sure this baby was healthy and strong.

She was also talking about trying to make a small space for the baby's bed and other items. She wanted the baby to feel loved and wanted and adored. She was counting down the weeks until the time for the birth arrived

Nellie Mae had discussed with Hank via letters that her search for a job was proving to be difficult. Hank suggested that she just stay home and help Bernie during the pregnancy and then with the baby after it was born. He thought it would be good practice for her to learn how to care for a baby before she was in the same situation herself.

CHAPTER THIRTEEN ~

One Saturday, Nellie Mae slept in. When she woke up she realized she hadn't seen Bernie the night before. She thought Bernie was probably tired and had fallen asleep early. Bernie had been especially exhausted after they worked on a nursery corner in her bedroom a couple of days ago. Maybe Bernie was sleeping in this morning. too.

She made some blueberry muffins and wrapped a few in a cloth napkin. She walked next door and knocked. Then she knocked again. She called out to Bernie.

"Bernie, it's Nellie Mae. Let me in. I have warm muffins to go with the orange juice in your refrigerator. Hurry up, the muffins are going to get cold. Open the door!" She laughed and knocked again.

The door lock turned and Bernie opened the door. She turned around and walked to the table. As Nellie Mae put the muffins down on the table she took a good look at Bernie.

"Oh my, Bernie! What's wrong? You look so pale. Is the morning sickness back again? Come lie down on the couch. Let me help you, sweetie."

Bernie burst into tears. "Oh, Nellie Mae. I lost the baby last night. I had a terrible pain during the night and I thought I had a stomach ache. But it was the worst pain I've ever had. I went into the bathroom and I must have fainted. When I came to, there was blood all over and a blob of something. I think it was the baby! Oh no, what am I going to do? Ed has been so excited about the baby, what am I going to do? How will I ever tell him? Oh Nellie Mae, help me please!" Bernie begged.

Nellie Mae just stood there. She couldn't comprehend what Bernie had just told her. "Are you in pain now, Bernie? Are you? Should we go to the base hospital or something?. What should I do? What can I do to help you? Oh, sweetie, I'm so sorry!"

Bernie sighed. "No, I am not in pain now. There isn't much bleeding since I last checked. It's kind of like having a period now. Just a little cramping and I am so tired. But I think I will be ok. I am actually hungry if you can believe that." Bernie dried her tears and then continued. "But...but what am I going to tell Ed? He is going to be so upset. He hasn't been happy because he has been away during the pregnancy and couldn't help me. Now he is going to blame himself for me." Bernie burst into tears again.

"Bernie, it's going to be alright. Ed would never blame you. Sure, he is going to be upset just like you are. But for now, you need to rest and get used to the idea that this has happened. I will help you as much as I can to deal with it. Do you want me to call your mother to come? What can I do for you?"

Bernie took a deep breath and answered. "No, I don't want to tell anyone right now. I need to think and figure out how to handle this the best way. For now, I don't even want to tell Ed. I need a few days to think it over. Please, just let me think. Ok, Nellie Mae?"

Nellie answered. " Of course, Sweetie. Do you want to eat something and then we can think about what to do next? I'll stay here tonight with you in case you need anything. After we eat, we can write letters if you feel up to it. How about that, Bernie?"

"Yes, let's eat and then maybe we can figure out what to do next. Thanks, Nellie Mae. I knew I could count on you." Bernie said to her friend.

Both the girls sat at the table and had a muffin and orange juice. They were each lost in thought and wondered why this had to happen.

CHAPTER FOURTEEN ~

Bernie decided to write to Ed and pretend like nothing had happened. She talked about being pregnant and what she was eating and how she was feeling. She told him all about the nursery that she and Nellie Mae had put together and promised to send photos of it very soon.

She felt terrible lying to her husband but she just didn't know how to break the news. She had to figure it out soon, though, because another photograph of her tummy should have been taken by now.

She told Ed that she had run out of film and had to get some at the PX the next time there was a supply available. Since sometimes items were out of stock at the PX for a few weeks, she though it would buy her some time before she had to tell him the truth.

In the meantime, Nellie Mae was having problems herself. It had been several days and Bernie was still in denial. Nellie Mae was worried about Bernie's state of mind. Bernie just didn't seem quite right. She didn't talk about the miscarriage and she didn't want to tell anyone that she had lost the baby. Bernie wasn't eating very much and Nellie Mae was trying to coax her into having a decent meal every day.

Bernie was wearing a sweater over her clothes to try to disguise that she wasn't any bigger this month. Nellie Mae knew that the truth had to come out very soon. Since she had promised not to tell anyone, Nellie Mae couldn't talk to her husband or her mother about what to do.

Another few weeks went by and Bernie still had not told anyone about the loss. Nellie Mae decided to have a serious talk with Bernie. And if Bernie didn't do anything about the situation, Nellie Mae was going to contact Bernie's mother for help. She didn't know what else to do.

She knew that when Ed found out; he was going to be devastated. She didn't want him to fall apart especially while he was overseas. She didn't know if the Red Cross could get him leave to come home and be with Bernie either.

Just as Nellie Mae had made up her mind to talk to Bernie and had practiced what she was going to say, there was a knock at the door. It was Bernie.

Bernie came in all excited. She seemed very upbeat. "I have an idea! This will fix everything. I just know it will work. And since you are my very best friend, I know I can count on you to make it happen!"

"What are you talking about, Bernie? Did you decide how to tell Ed about the miscarriage? Did you talk to your mother about it?" Nellie Mae asked.

"Oh no, I don't need to do any of that, Nellie Mae. I figured out how to do this and all I need is you. Well, I need you and I need my brother-in-law's help. Wait until I tell you what I figured out. Just wait. I know this is going to work. Especially since Ed won't be coming home for several more months anyway." Bernie said excitedly.

"What do you mean that all you need is me and your brother-in-law? You are not making any sense, Bernie. Sit down and take a deep breath and then explain what you are talking about, please." Nellie Mae sputtered.

Bernie sat down at the table. " Ok, let me explain. I have been thinking about this for days now. I have it all worked out too. What I need is for you to have my baby! You get pregnant and have the baby for me. Ed will think it is ours and Hank will never know. Neither of them will be coming home for several months anyway so it's perfect! The baby will be already be here and they won't know how old he really is. If he isn't crawling or even walking and talking, we will just tell them he is just a bit small for his age. I've been told that first babies are usually smaller than the next ones that come along anyway."

"I know we can do this, Nellie Mae. I know it! It will work. You'll see! And all you have to do is get pregnant and have the baby for me. For Ed and me. You won't have to take care of the baby at all. Just have it for me, please, please, Nellie Mae! I'm begging you."

"What! What? I can't have your baby. How is that going to happen? I can't get pregnant without a man... Oh wait. Are you actually going to ask me to sleep with your brother-in-law to get pregnant?"

"You can't be serious! I can't do that! I could never do that! How could you ask me to even consider it?

I love Hank only and I would never betray him in that way. You can't ask me to do that! You can't, Bernie! I love you and I would do anything for you but I just can't do that. No, No, NO!" Nellie Mae shouted.

"Wait, Nellie Mae. Wait a minute! You didn't let me finish. I'm not asking you to sleep with my brother-in-law. Of course not! I've been researching this. There's another way. All it takes some of his sperm and you. You don't even have to see each other."

"Ed's brother is stationed in another state. He is in the Navy and he will be on leave next month. He said he would come here for a visit. He said he would do it. Then he is back overseas and won't be stateside for months. He doesn't intend to come back here at all any way. He thinks he is doing it for me. He thinks I want to use his sperm and get pregnant again. That way the baby might resemble Ed's family members."

"He said he won't have anything to do with the baby after it is born either. He said he was willing to do whatever I needed to get through this loss of my baby. He said he would never tell anyone. He won't even have to meet you or even see you."

Nellie Mae laughed nervously. "What do you mean, he won't have to meet me or see me. What are we going to do ~ have a curtain between us when we do that. Oh ugh! I can't even say the words. Bernie, I love you like my sister but I just can't. Please don't ask me again. I just can't be with any other man."

"But you don't have to BE with him. Let me explain. I was reading that all you need is fresh sperm inserted into your body. We can use a turkey baster. I will have my brother-in-law in my living room and I will bring the sperm in the baster into my bedroom and help you put it inside you. He won't even know you are in there. He said he would leave as soon as I go into the bedroomto give me privacy. I know it sounds crazy but I do think it will work."

"Please, Nellie Mae. Just think about it and let me know if you will even consider it. Please, I am begging you. I would do it for you, I would!" Bernie grabbed Nellie Mae's shoulders and looked her right in the eyes.

"Oh Bernie. I do love you and I know you would do it for me if I asked. But I just don't know if I can do it. I don't even know if I would get pregnant. What if I didn't get pregnant? How long does it take to know if I got pregnant?" Nellie Mae questioned.

"Well, if my brother-in-law came right at the beginning of his leave, he could be here several days and we could try it several times. Then, if you don't get pregnant…Well, I guess I will just have to tell Ed I lost his baby." Bernie burst into tears.

"Please, Nellie Mae, you are my only hope and the only one I could ever ask to share this secret. I think it is too soon for me to try to get pregnant again right now. What if I lost another baby anyway? I couldn't handle losing another child!" Bernie cried.

Nellie Mae took a deep breath and sighed. "I don't know, Bernie. I just don't know. Let me pray about it and I will give you an answer in a couple of days."

Nellie Mae walked home and sat in her rocking chair. What am I going to do now? She thought. How can I do this and betray my husband? Would I be betraying my wedding vows? Is this the right thing to do? Would it work? Could it be possible? I just don't know. I guess I need to write a list of pros and cons right now and then sleep on it. I'll look at the list tomorrow morning after I have prayed about it and try to decide then.

Back at Bernie's house, she was praying as well. She just knew this was the answer and it would work. If Nellie Mae didn't get pregnant or refused to even try, Bernie didn't know if she could go on living. She hadn't told Nellie Mae that she was afraid to get pregnant herself again. She didn't want to lose another baby. But even worse, she knew she didn't want to live without a child.

CHAPTER FIFTEEN ~

Nellie Mae tossed and turned all night. If she fell asleep for a few minutes, she had bad dreams about babies and Hank being angry with her. She didn't know what to do. She loved Bernie as much as a real sister and she did want to help her. But there had to be another way. Why did Bernie ask her to make such a difficult decision? It just wasn't fair.

She stayed inside her house all day. When the mailman came, he knocked at her door. He had a small package that she had to sign for. It was from Hank. She couldn't make out the postmark but it was obvious that he had sent it through the military mail system because of all the strange stamps and marks on the box. She opened it up.

Inside was a beautifully delicate necklace with a heart on it. As she examined it carefully, she could see that the locket could open. She slowly opened it up and saw the face of her handsome husband with a big smile on his face.

Inside the package was a letter too.

My dearest darling wife:

I was able to get into a town near where we are temporarily stationed. It had a tiny little jewelry store and the jeweler makes these precious little lockets. I decided to buy one for you and put my photo inside. That way you can wear it and keep me close to your heart every day.

I love you so much. I miss you almost more than I can say. I can't wait until this war is over and I can come back to you. I'm not sure when that will be but I am praying every night that it will be sooner than later.

Please always know that I adore you, my darling one. All my love is for you.

Hank

PS. You may not get my letters for a few days because we are going out again. I am writing every day so you will probably get several letters in one bundle when they can be mailed out.

*****

Nellie Mae folded up the letter and quickly put the locket around her neck. She said a prayer that Hank would be safe until he was able to come home again.

CHAPTER SIXTEEN ~

Nellie Mae started to cry. Oh, Hank, how I wish you were here with me too. I need to talk to you so much. I really wish I could tell you what has happened with Bernie and the baby. I know you could tell me what to do, what is best for everyone. But I can't tell anyone...ever. Whether I do this for Bernie or not, I can't tell anyone that she ever asked me to have a baby for her. What am I going to do?

There was a knock at the door. Nellie Mae tried to ignore it but then she heard Bernie calling. "Let me in, Nellie Mae. Please, I have to talk to you right now!"

Nellie Mae opened the door. She said "Bernie, I haven't decided yet. I haven't been able to sleep all night trying to figure out what is right to do. I want to help you, I really do. It's just...oh I don't know..it just doesn't seem right. I expected my first pregnancy to be Hank's baby and mine. I don't know how I would feel about having someone else's baby for them. It just doesn't make sense to me. I can't decide."

Bernie interrupted her. "But you HAVE to do this! YOU HAVE TO! I can't tell Ed that the baby is gone. He won't be able to take that kind of news when he is in a war, in danger of dying. He just wrote me a letter about how all that keeps him going is thinking about me being pregnant. He said he can't wait to come home and meet his son. He is positive it is a boy. He wants to name him Edison Bernard. That way the baby will have both of our names! Isn't that a great idea? I love it! So just say Yes, please, Nellie Mae, please."

Nellie Mae signed deeply. "Bernie, I need to think about this more. I'm going to take the bus into town and find a church. I want to talk to a minister or a priest who doesn't know me."

"I want to ask if I should do something for my very best friend in the world that might hurt other people if they find out. I really feel I need some guidance from someone who doesn't know the circumstances. I will talk to you about it tomorrow." Nellie Mae said to her.

Bernie asked "Should I go with you? I could explain why I asked this of you. I could make the minister understand. I know I could!"

"Please let me go too! Please! You don't know how important this is to me. I'm desperate, Nellie Mae. If you don't agree to do this, I don't know what I will do. I can't disappoint Ed. Not now, not ever!"

"And if you don't do it, I will never be your friend AGAIN! I won't speak to you or acknowledge you. I'll just disappear one day and no one will be able to find me and it will be all your fault too!" And with that, Bernie walked out the door and slammed it behind her.

Nellie Mae was really worried about Bernie's state of mind. Bernie looked like she hadn't slept or brushed her hair in days. In fact, her clothes were dirty and wrinkled too. Nellie Mae wondered how stable Bernie was. Maybe she would lose her mind if Nellie Mae didn't agree. What was she going to do?

Nellie Mae took a bath and got dressed. She had just enough time to get to the bus stop for the next bus to town. When she got off the bus. She looked in the telephone book for churches. She found one just a block away and started walking towards it.

When she arrived, she quietly went into the sanctuary . She knelt down to pray and tried to focus on what she was going to say. She realized the church was Catholic when she saw a priest walk by. He entered a small booth and she noticed other people walking into the booth for a few moments and then coming out to pray.

She got in line and waited for her turn. As she opened the door, she could see the silhouette of a man on the other side of a small screened area. She sat down and waited.

The priest asked her to make her confession. Nellie Mae stammered that she wasn't Catholic but she had a problem and wondered if she could talk to the priest.

He said "Of course. Please tell me what is on your mind. Just say it the best way you can explain it and I will see what I can offer you as guidance. Please begin."

Nellie Mae folded her hands and closed her eyes and bowed her head. "Father, I don't know what to do. My dearest friend in all the world…someone I have grown up with has asked me to do something for her that I don't think I should do. I want to help her because she is desperate but I just don't know if I can do it."

"She is my best friend. Her husband and mine are in the military and they are overseas now, fighting in the war. All four of us were married just a few months ago. She found out that she was pregnant shortly after her husband, Ed...I mean her husband left for his assignment. He was thrilled and has already named the baby because he is sure it is going to be a boy."

The priest said "That's wonderful. But I don't understand the problem. Doesn't your friend want to have a baby? Is she frightened of having it while her husband is away? What's wrong?"

Nellie Mae continued. "Oh no, Father, she wants to have the baby. Well, she did. She...um...she lost the baby a couple of weeks ago. She is so upset."

"She is clearly not thinking rationally. She doesn't want to tell her husband because she is afraid he will not be able to handle the news while he is so far away."

The priest asked "Has she told him or contacted the Red Cross? They might be able to arrange a phone call or even break the news to him there. What about her family? Can't they help her?"

"Oh no, Father!" Nellie Mae continued. "She won't tell anyone. She only told me because I went to her door when I hadn't seen her for a day. She was exhausted and almost inconsolable. She just cried and cried."

"I got her to eat some food and drink some tea and she fell asleep on her couch. I stayed with her all night. She told me not to tell anyone and she didn't want to go to the base hospital either. I just don't know what to do now."

The priest asked "Why? Is she still weak or sick? Does she need to see a doctor?"

Nellie Mae bowed her head again. "Father, she has asked me to do something that I don't think I can do for her. She wants me to have a baby for her."

"I told her I couldn't break my wedding vows with my husband. She swears she would never tell him or her husband and will pretend the baby is hers. She thinks by the time our husbands come home again, the baby will be walking or even talking and her husband will never know the difference."

"But, but how does she think you could get pregnant? Surely she doesn't want you to sleep with another man…to betray your own husband! The child would be a bastard at the very least. Conceived in sin in any case. It's an impossible request. Obviously she isn't in her right state of mind! Is she a Catholic? Doesn't she need to talk to her own priest? I understand why you are so confused and upset about this request, my dear." the priest said quietly.

"Yes, Father." Nellie Mae answered. "I am deeply troubled about this. No, she isn't Catholic and she hasn't talked to any minister either. She just got this idea in her head and she won't let it go."

"She said her brother-in-law said he would help her. She thinks she can bring his….um..*bodily fluid* into her bedroom and use a turkey baster that I would…um...put inside me?"

"I'm sorry, Father, for speaking so indelicately but that IS what she wants to do."

"She said the brother-in-law thinks she will be the one who gets pregnant. She isn't going to let him see me in her bedroom. She said I won't know what he looks like either. He's in another branch of the service and will be leaving in about a month or so for duty. He doesnt live around here so he won't be coming back here. He is willing to come here for a few days on his last leave before shipping out."

"I...I just don't know what to do, Father. I love her like a sister and I'm worried about what she might do if I refuse. She isn't acting like herself at all. I'm scared she will hurt herself."

"Well, this is a dilemma" the priest replied. I don't know of what Scriptures I can turn to for guidance right now. I need to do some praying myself and see if I can find some answers for you."

The priest paused in thought and then said "Of course, there IS that story in the Bible..., Genesis, Chapter 16. Abraham and his barren wife, Sarah wanted so much to have a child. Sarah felt ashamed because she couldn't give Abraham a son. So Sarah told her servant, Hagar, to go to

Abraham. Hagar does get pregnant with his child but when she delivers the child, she doesn't want to give it up. There's the dilemma of the child having three parents. The husband and wife and the surrogate."

The priest continued "I understand that you love this woman. Do you think she could accept this child if it wasn't really from her body? I'm concerned about the sins upon the child when it is born if it is conceived in this way. I need to ponder on this a bit. Can you come back again?"

Nellie Mae said "I'm not sure how much time I have to give her an answer. If I am agreeable, she has to contact her brother-in-law about his leave."

"If I refuse...I just don't know what will happen to her. I would not want to tell her husband that she did something to herself because she lost the baby. I don't know what answer is the right one. I just don't know."

The priest told Nellie Mae if she would come back in another week, he would try to have something to help her make the decision. Personally, he didn't think she should grant the request from her friend. But he also knew that Nellie Mae was trying to do what was best for everyone involved and especially for her friend.

Nellie Mae caught the next bus back to the base. At least she had all night to rethink all the options because she would have to tell Bernie something the next morning. Knowing Bernie, she would be knocking at the door as soon as the sun came up.

CHAPTER SEVENTEEN ~

Nellie Mae spent another sleepless night. She rocked in her chair, she prayed, she drank tea and she make a list of the pros and cons. Nothing seemed to help. She just didn't know what to do. She was extremely worried about Bernie. She wondered if Hank would understand if she ever had to tell him her decision.

It was barely light when Nellie Mae heard a soft knock at her door. She opened it and saw Bernie standing there. Bernie looked more haggard than before. She was exhausted and her face was swollen from all the tears she had shed since she lost the baby. She grabbed Nellie Mae's hand and asked "Did you decide? Will you do it? Please, Nellie Mae, please."

"I'm so scared of how I'm feeling. This morning, I found myself holding a bottle of Ed's pain pills when he had a tooth pulled and I was actually thinking of taking them. I'm afraid of what I might do if you refuse. Please, Nellie Mae. I need your help now!" Bernie burst into tears again.

Nellie Mae put her arms about Bernie's trembling body. She walked Bernie over to the couch and covered her shaking body with a quilt. She went to the kitchen and made some tea for both of them.

She knew what she had to do. She couldn't let Bernie down and she would have to keep this secret for the rest of her life. She could never tell Hank or Ed or anyone else for that matter. She would have to avoid seeing her family when she started to show if she got pregnant. She didn't like keeping secrets from her loved ones but she had no choice. She had to save Bernie.

So Nellie Mae sat down beside Bernie and asked her. "Tell me again how this will work. You are sure that your brother-in-law won't see me or know that I am going to carry this child, right? You promise? And if I don't get pregnant after this, you won't ask me again, right? I don't think I could keep on doing this, breaking my wedding vows over and over. I just don't! Bernie, you HAVE to promise me that you won't ever tell anyone. You'll have to continue to wear heavy sweaters so you look pregnant for awhile."

Bernie grabbed Nellie Mae's arm. "Does that mean that you WILL do it for me? Oh please, say you will!

I promise not to ever tell. I promise to do whatever you say. I promise to help you through the pregnancy and I'll never, EVER forget this, Nellie Mae. I love you so much." Bernie burst into tears and grabbed Nellie Mae in a huge hug.

CHAPTER EIGHTEEN ~

Bernie came over every day to be sure that Nellie Mae was eating plenty of good food. She brought her all kinds of treats too. She offered to give Nellie Mae extra money when she started to see a doctor. They decided that Nellie Mae would go into town to see a doctor and use another name. When she was ready to deliver, she would check into the hospital under that name. She would say her husband was overseas. And Bernie would accompany her to all the appointments so she could follow the pregnancy all the way through.

Bernie came over one morning with more exciting news. Her brother-in-law was on his way. He had leave for 2 weeks and would stay in town so no one would wonder why he was hanging around the base. Bernie assured him that she didn't expect anything from him when the pregnancy was confirmed. She told him that she would be fine with keeping his identity a secret.

When he finally arrived, he called Bernie to ask when he should come to visit. She set the time and made sure that Nellie Mae was aware as well.

That evening, Nellie Mae waited in Bernie's bedroom in her bed. Nellie Mae felt so embarrassed and so ashamed about what she was about to do. But she had decided she would do it for her best friend and she was going to follow through.

She heard a soft knock at Bernie's door and some quiet talking. Bernie came into the bedroom and said that she was giving her brother-in-law some privacy while he prepared himself for the task. He was going to knock on the bedroom door when he was done and Bernie would take the cup and use the turkey baster to transfer it to Nellie Mae.

It wasn't long before the knock came. Bernie slightly opened the door, took the cup and quickly put the turkey baster in it. She handed the baster to Nellie Mae and turned her back to give Nellie Mae some privacy. Nellie Mae did what she was told to do. She transferred the liquid and then laid in the bed with her legs up on a pillow for about an hour. She felt so ashamed. Bernie had gone out into the living room to give Nellie Mae some time alone. Nellie Mae heard Bernie say goodbye to her brother-in-law and shut the front door.

Nellie Mae felt like she had betrayed Hank. She didn't know if she could ever forgive herself. And she realized that this might be the first of many transfers in the next 2 weeks. She took a deep breath and said a prayer for forgiveness. After she had composed herself and dried her tears, she got up and went out to the living room. She asked Bernie when her brother-in-law would be coming back again.

Bernie replied "He said he would come every evening when it is dark. So for two weeks, I guess. I'm sorry, Nellie Mae, I know this is very difficult for you and I am so grateful to you."

CHAPTER NINETEEN ~

The nightly visits continued every night for 2 weeks. Nellie Mae got used to the procedure and hardly thought about it at all. It was easier to put it out of her mind and think of other more pleasant things.

She made up grocery lists in her head. She did multiplication tables. She spelled words. She wrote letters to her family while she laid quietly in Bernie's bed for an hour every night. But finally, it was over. Nellie Mae was so relieved. She was working hard to keep her mind on other things. She didn't want to talk about it with Bernie at all.

Life slowly got back to a new normal for the friends. They didn't feel so awkward with each other and started to smile and enjoy each other's company again. They started cooking and baking new recipes. They found new recipes and shared their allotments of sugar and coffee and tea.

They were learning to knit and they each worked on sweaters and socks for their husbands. Even if the clothing wasn't perfect, at least it was warm and made with plenty of love.

They continued to exchange letters with Ed and Hank. Bernie kept up a correspondence about being pregnant. She even stuffed a pillow under her dress for photographs so she looked like she was getting bigger.

One evening, Bernie brought over some spaghetti and meatballs for dinner. Just as they sat down to eat, Nellie Mae took one look at the sauce and her face went white. She felt dizzy and grabbed the chair.

"What's wrong, Nellie Mae?" Bernie quickly asked.

"I don't know. I just felt kind of dizzy and sick. I hope I am not coming down with a cold or something. I just need to stay seated for a minute. Could you bring me a glass of water, please? And move this food, it's making me feel sicker." Nellie Mae said as she put her head down on the table.

"Here's the water and a cold cloth for your head, Nellie Mae. Are you feeling better now? Do you want to lie down on the couch for a few minutes?" Bernie asked.

"No, I think I am feeling better. I wonder what brought that on. I was feeling fine earlier today. It was the smell of that spaghetti sauce and the look of the meatballs that bothered me." Nellie Mae remarked.

Bernie took a long look at Nellie Mae. "Um, Nellie Mae, have you had your monthly visit from Aunt Flo lately?"

"Of course, I mark it on the calendar every month. I think it was just a few weeks ago. Maybe that is what is wrong with me." Nellie Mae got up to check the calendar. She kept looking at it and checking back. "Oh my! It's been more weeks than I thought. Aunt Flo hasn't been here since…oh my…since right before your brother-in-law was here. Do you suppose I could be pregnant?" Nellie Mae whispered.

Bernie's face got a glow. Her cheeks turned pink and she smiled. "Maybe you are, Nellie Mae! That would be so wonderful. Maybe we should wait a few more weeks and then if nothing has happened, we can find a doctor in town and make sure. Oh I hope it's true! It will be the answer and the miracle I have been praying for."

Nellie Mae's face turned white again. "Oh my. I don't know what to think. This isn't how I expected to find out I might be pregnant. But I guess we will know in a few more weeks, won't we?"

Bernie replied. "I can't wait. I hope it is a little boy because that is what my Ed wants. But if it turns out to be a baby girl, I'm fine with that too. I just want a baby to take care of and to dress up and love. Whatever you need to get through this time, you know I will be there for you, night or day."

CHAPTER TWENTY~

The days seemed to fly by for Nellie Mae. She was having a strange reaction to this new situation. On one hand, she was excited to see how Bernie was getting back to normal. Bernie had a new sparkle in her eyes and she was full of energy. She had so many things to do that she could hardly sit still for more than five minutes.

She was constantly bringing food over for Nellie Mae. Custards and oatmeal cookies, homemade vegetable soup and bread. Nellie Mae was worried that if she was not pregnant, she would gain all this weight because she was eating so much. And what would happen to Bernie if this was just a false alarm?

Nellie Mae seems to be fortunate with the pregnancy. She didn't have morning sickness at all. Sometimes she felt a big queasy in the evening but once she ate, she was fine. She had just a few cravings. She wanted fried eggs and bacon every morning and an apple.

On the other hand, Nellie Mae felt so guilty. She had broken her wedding vows to her husband. She just couldn't get past that. She found it harder to write him a letter every day. Just as he had told her when he sent the gold locket, his letters had stopped. She wasn't too worried about that because all the other wives said the same thing. So she just tried to stay optimistic and take care of herself.

When she noticed that the waistband on her skirts and dresses were getting a bit tight, she decided she should visit a doctor in town. She told Bernie she had made an appointment and asked if Bernie wanted to go with her. Of course, Bernie jumped at the chance.

Bernie said she wanted to experience the pregnancy all the way through so if Ed asked about it, she could tell him how she had felt and what labor was like and delivery and so on. She was writing a journal too. She just used different dates when she wrote in it so when he read it after he came home, it would appear that the first pregnancy was a success.

The doctor appointment day finally arrived. Nellie Mae was really nervous. She had no idea what to say about who she was and where her husband was. She decided to just make up a name and say she was visiting her cousin and decided to see a doctor while she was in the area. If she was pregnant, she would make up an excuse that she was staying with her cousin for the entire pregnancy because her husband was in the service overseas.

Nellie Mae and Bernie met the doctor and they both felt very comfortable with him. He checked Nellie Mae over and said he was sure she was pregnant. And he gave her a due date. He reminded her to get plenty of rest and eat as well as she could. He told her he didn't foresee any problems and he thought the delivery would go very well. He said he could come to her cousin's home to deliver the baby if necessary but he thought being in the hospital, especially for the first baby was a better plan.

Nellie Mae vowed to follow all his advice and made another appointment for 6 weeks later. He gave her some pamphlets to read about childbirth and care for an infant. She was going to do everything right to make sure this pregnancy went well and then she could give the baby to Bernie and try to put how the baby came out of her head. She knew it would be several long months before this was over but she really hoped the time would go by quickly.

CHAPTER TWENTY ONE ~

As the weeks went by, Bernie continued to cook special meals for Nellie Mae. She also sewed some bigger skirts and tops for Nellie Mae to cover up her change in condition. Nellie Mae wore a heavy sweater almost all the time. She stayed inside most of the day and only ventured out when it was getting dark. Many times Bernie picked up any groceries Nellie Mae needed from the PX or in town.

Nellie Mae was settling into a routine and starting to feel better. She liked the feeling of the small bump that she could rest her hands on. She was getting used to feeling the little flutters and then kicks of the baby. At times, she imagined it was her baby and Hank's that she was carrying. She could hardly wait to be pregnant for their own family .

She had her next appointment and the doctor was pleased with the outcome. She hadn't gained too much weight and she was feeling very good. The doctor made the next appointment for a second trimester checkup. He thought she would be near the beginning of her 5th month by then.

He told her to continue just as she had been doing and if she had any unusual symptoms to contact his office immediately.

CHAPTER TWENTY TWO ~

Nellie Mae had been daydreaming and resting on her couch one afternoon before she started dinner. Suddenly Bernie came rushing over and screamed for Nellie Mae to open the door.

When Nellie Mae got to the door, Bernie took one look at her, stepped into the house and fainted on the floor. Nellie Mae awkwardly got down on her knees and tried to wake Bernie up . When Bernie finally opened her eyes, she looked like she had seen a ghost.

"What's wrong, Bernie?" Nellie asked anxiously. "What in the world happened, why were you screaming? Please tell me!"

"Oh, I can't believe this is happening to me. Not now! Not after all I have gone through for these past few months. I can't take it. I just can't! What am I going to do now? Oh, help me please, Nellie Mae! Help me to understand it all." Bernie wailed.

"You have to tell me what is wrong, Bernie." Nellie Mae replied. "What has happened to cause you to fall apart like this. I haven't seen you this upset since you lost your own baby. What is it?"

Bernie opened her hand and a piece of wadded up paper fell on the floor. It was a telegram.

Nellie Mae picked it up and asked Bernie. "Do you want me to read this? Is this what has caused you to be so upset?"

Bernie whispered. "Just read it. And then tell me what it says. I know I didn't read it properly and this is all a bad dream. Please tell me what it says and that it is good news, not bad please. I'm begging you."

Nellie Mae carefully smoothed the telegram so she could read the printed words.

****
Dear Mrs. Dawson:

The United States Government along with the Branch of the Army must regretfully report to you that your husband, Sgt. Edison Dawson, was caught in a surprise attack against the Allied Forces a few days ago.

The battle became one of the costliest in terms of casualties for the United States thus far.

Sgt Dawson was instrumental in saving several of his comrades because he stayed behind to keep shooting at the enemy while his unit retreated to safer ground.

Sgt Edison Dawson died a hero. His remains have been retrieved and his body will be returned to the United States as soon as possible for a military burial.

Our deepest sympathies to you and your family.

**President and Commander In Chief
Harry S. Truman**

******

Nellie Mae quietly sat down and bowed her head in prayer. "Oh, Bernie. What can I do or say? Do you want me to contact your parents? Talk to me, Bernie."

Bernie raised her tear streaked face and shuddered. She finally whispered. "I don't know what to do. My family still thinks I'm pregnant. I guess I could tell them I'm too far along to travel. But knowing them, they will want to come here."

Or, I guess I could tell them that I lost the baby when I got the news about Ed. Would that be wrong to lie about the timing of the miscarriage? Oh, what am I going to do? "

Suddenly Bernie looked directly at Nellie Mae. "Oh my, Nellie Mae, you didn't get a telegram too, did you? I couldn't bear it if Hank was wounded in that fight so far away from us. Surely if he had been hurt or worse, you would have heard by now." Bernie said.

Nellie Mae took a deep breath. "No, I haven't heard anything. But I wonder if the Chaplain has. Maybe he has a list of the wounded or killed soldiers and can fill us in. Let's walk over to the Chapel or his office and check. I imagine, by now, a lot of other wives in the same unit on the base are wondering the same thing."

Nellie Mae helped Bernie to her feet. They put on their coats and hats and walked to the Chapel. There were many people inside praying and talking quietly. No one had any more news to share. But then the Chaplain came into the sanctuary and asked for quiet while he read a statement.

The official statement said there were a few more soldiers who had been wounded from Ed and Hank's unit. Ed was the only one who had been killed. Everyone gathered around Bernie to give her their sympathies.

Bernie and Nellie Mae left the chapel and walked back home. They had a lot of things to discuss and they had to make a new plan. Now that Ed wasn't coming home, Bernie didn't have to lie any longer about when the baby was born. That should make the rest of Nellie Mae's pregnancy a little less stressful.

For the next couple of days, Bernie didn't come over. Nellie Mae thought Bernie probably needed some time alone. Nellie Mae did insist that Bernie come to the door so she could give her some food to eat. Bernie still hadn't decided what to tell her parents. She said she needed a little time to think about all of it before she called them.

Nellie Mae was trying to give Bernie time to sort out her feelings. But Nellie Mae was very worried about Bernie's state of mind. She wasn't acting as energetic as before. Her appearance was shockingly like it was after the miscarriage. She seemed to be in a fog. She didn't respond when

Nellie Mae brought food over. By the looks of the cold and congealed plates of food still sitting on the table, Bernie wasn't eating too much either.

After another week went by, Nellie Mae felt like she had to confront Bernie. She walked over to Bernie's house and knocked at the door.

Bernie finally answered. She looked like she hadn't bathed or slept in days. Her hair was stringy and dirty. Her face was pale with dark circles under her eyes. She was extremely quiet as she let Nellie Mae into the house. She sat on the couch and just slumped over with her hands over her eyes.

Nellie Mae waited a moment and then she said. "Bernie, we need to talk. I'm entering my last 3 months of this pregnancy. I need your help more than ever."

"I want you to start to prepare for the baby coming home to you . We've worked together and made a place for him to sleep in your bedroom with you. Now we need to finish up. We need to make diapers and get bottles and formula and figure out what else we will need for the baby. What do you want to do first?"

Then Nellie Mae took another deep breath and said "And then you need to tell your parents because you will not be able to live here on the base much longer since Ed is…..um….since Ed has passed." Nellie Mae said as she put her arms around Bernie.

Bernie looked up and shook her head. "I don't know. I don't know! I don't think I can do this. What's the point anyway? Ed is dead! The baby has no father now. I don't think I can raise a baby on my own without any help. I don't think I even want to see this baby….ever!" Bernie covered her face with her hands.

Nellie Mae's mouth fell open. "What are you talking about, Bernie? You begged me over and over to have a baby for you and Ed. You said you had to have a baby for him to come home to. I know losing Ed has been a shock and will be difficult for you for a long time."

"But you have a responsibility to this baby that you prayed for. You HAVE to take this baby when it's born. I can't raise it! How would I explain how I had a baby when Hank has been gone for so long? What do you mean, you don't want the baby now! You planned this whole thing and now you HAVE to follow through and finish the plan! I can't keep the baby. I could never explain to Hank why I had the baby. I can't lie anymore." Nellie Mae explained.

Bernie burst into tears. "Oh, I know. IT'S ALL MY FAULT! I'm being punished for the lie. I should have told Ed that I lost our baby when it happened. But I didn't and now look what a mess we are in. Oh, Nellie Mae, I don't know what to do. Will you give me a few more days to make new plans, please?"

Nellie Mae gave Bernie a hug. She said "Yes, of course, I will, Bernie. I know this is a terrible shock and you need some rest and some food to get stronger. Why dont you go home and take a hot bath and wash your hair? I'll fix a nice dinner and we can eat and talk this evening. Dinner will be ready in about 3 hours. That will give you time to take a nap too."

Bernie slowly got up off the couch. She started towards the door and then stopped and turned to Nellie Mae. "You are so kind to me. You have always tried to be there for me and I know you always will. I'm sorry I got us into this situation. I'll do some thinking and come up with a new plan. I love you and I always will, my sweet Nellie Mae. Please always remember how much I love you." Bernie walked down the steps and started for her home.

Nellie Mae called out to her. "Remember, dinner will be ready in 3 hours. Come over as soon as you can."

Bernie waved her hand and very slowly walked up her own steps into her house. She shut the door and closed all the curtains inside.

CHAPTER TWENTY THREE ~

Nellie Mae decided to make a hardy beef stew so it could simmer while she also took a short nap. She settled down on the couch after starting a warm fire. She put her favorite quilt over her and felt herself sinking into a dream.

When Nellie Mae woke up, the fire was nearly out. The room was dark. She could smell the stew and jumped up to check that it had not burned. She added some liquid and stirred it. Where was Bernie? Did she fall asleep and just not wake up yet? Nellie Mae decided to give Bernie a few more minutes.

When Bernie did not show up after Nellie Mae had waited another half-hour, Nellie Mae turned the flame under the stew down very low and walked to Bernie's house. She knocked at the door but got no answer. She knocked loudly and called Bernie's name. Still no response.

She took out the key that Bernie had given her to keep for emergencies and opened the door. She called out to Bernie but there was no answer.

She heard the sound of water so she went towards the bathroom. " Bernie, are you in the tub? Did you fall asleep in there?"

Then Nellie Mae stepped in a puddle of water seeping from under the bathroom door. She quickly opened the door and saw water spilling over the top of the tub.

Inside the tub was Bernie. She was under water. There was a pill bottle floating in the water too. There were no pills inside the bottle.

Bernie was dead.

CHAPTER TWENTY FOUR ~

Nellie Mae was in shock. Now what was she going to do? What should she say to Bernie's parents about what happened? They could probably believe that Bernie took her life because Ed had been killed in the war but how could Nellie Mae explain why Bernie wasn't pregnant any longer? Should she tell them that Bernie lost the baby several weeks ago and was so depressed that she didn't want to tell anyone? Well, yes, that could also explain why she chose to take her life after Ed was killed.

But how could Nellie Mae explain why SHE was pregnant? Wait, maybe she should talk to the Chaplain and suggest that Bernie's body be taken back home along with Ed's body when it was shipped back. Then the parents could bury them together and Nellie Mae could avoid going back home.

Yes, that was it. She only hoped that the Chaplain would be able to make it happen. She had better run to his office right now and tell him to come to

Bernie's house. Or...wait, she would call him and ask him to come over. She couldn't bear the idea of leaving Bernie alone in the house even though she was dead.

Nellie Mae got on the phone and called. Thankfully the Chaplain was in his office. Nellie Mae was crying as she explained the reason for the call.

"Oh, Chaplain, please come to Bernie Dawson's home immediately. I've been so worried about her since she heard that Ed had been killed. I came over to check on her because she was supposed to come to my house for dinner. She didn't answer the door so I used the key she gave me."

Nellie Mae took a deep breath and then said "I just found her bo....I just found her body in the tub. She's dead! There was a pill bottle in the water. Oh please, come right away. I don't know what to do next."

The Chaplain rushed over. He brought the Base Commander with him. They checked for a pulse even though they knew there wasn't one.

Nellie Mae was sitting in the living room, wrapped up in a quilt to hide her pregnancy and she felt sick inside.

Finally the men returned to the living room to talk with Nellie Mae.

"It's obvious that she lost her senses because of her husband's death. We will contact her parents as they are now her next of kin. Do you have any idea why she took Ed's death so hard, Nellie Mae?"

Nellie Mae wiped her eyes and looked up. "Well, something else had happened a few months ago. She wouldn't talk to anyone but me...not even her husband. She lost the baby she was expecting. She was afraid if she told Ed that he would fall apart while he was overseas. She was trying to figure out what to do but she never really got over that loss. Then she got the telegram that Ed had been killed overseas. I guess it was just too much for her to take."

Nellie Mae then added "I wonder if it would be easier for her parents if her body could be taken back home for a funeral. And is there anyway that

Ed's remains could be shipped there too so they can be buried together? What do you think, Chaplain?. Is that something that is possible for the Army to do for Captain Dawson and his wife "

The Chaplain looked at the Base Commander who nodded his head. "Yes, I think that can be arranged. I will telephone her parents when I get back to my office and work out the details. Are you planning on going home too for the funeral, Nellie Mae? We can probably find a way to get you back home too."

Nellie Mae paused before she answered. "Well, I was thinking that I should pack up her belongings and have them shipped home to her parents. I know you will want the unit now that Ed is no longer a member of the service. So I think Bernie would have wanted me to go through her things instead of any one else. Would that be allowable, Chaplain?"

The Chaplain looked at the Base Commander once again. With the agreement in place with a nod from him, the Chaplain told Nellie Mae that would be very helpful. He would have some boxes brought over for packing. He told her she had a week to get the unit all cleaned out. But if she needed more time, it would be arranged.

Nellie Mae said she would get to work on it right away and let them know when she was finished. She asked if she could go to her own home before Bernie's body was removed. The men agreed that would be best.

Nellie Mae walked home. As she entered her house, she smelled the stew. It was burnt. She turned off the flame and scraped the burned meal into the trash. She didn't feel hungry at all. She fixed a cup of tea and sat in her rocking chair.

Tomorrow she would start to clean out Bernie's house. She couldn't believe Bernie was gone. She had lost her dearest friend in the entire world. And what would she do without Bernie to talk with?

She kept rocking in her chair and drinking the hot tea. She closed her eyes for a moment and fell asleep. When she woke up, she remembered with a feeling of sadness that Bernie was gone. Then she thought of something else. Something even more frightening!

She was pregnant with Bernie's baby! She was having a baby and had no explanation for it. How was she going to explain to Hank? What was she going to do now?

She remembered she had another doctor appointment in the next week. Maybe she should talk about giving the baby up for adoption. She could tell the doctor that her husband wasn't coming home. She didn't want to say he was killed because she was superstitious. She would have to look into adoption because there was nothing else she could do. It would be best for the baby.

CHAPTER TWENTY FIVE ~

Nellie Mae kept very busy during the next few days packing up Bernie's possessions. She felt a pang of sadness when she saw all the letters from Ed that Bernie had tied up in a blue ribbon. She even found an unfinished letter Bernie had started for Ed. She quickly put all of them in a box and sealed it up. She wrote PERSONAL LETTERS on the box.

She went through Bernie's clothes and picked out a few of the maternity outfits Bernie had worn during her own pregnancy. Nellie Mae thought she would feel closer to Bernie if she wore some of the outfits.

It took her about three days to pack up everything. She mopped the floors and cleaned the rest of the little home. Then she called the Chaplain to tell him she had finished the job. She told him she didn't want to go back into Bernie's unit. It just hurt too much. She left the extra key on the kitchen table and closed the door.

The next day was her doctor's appointment. She got on the bus and then walked to the doctor's office. When she was in the examination room, the doctor came in.

"How are you doing today, Mrs. Smythe? Any problems? Any unusual things that you want to talk about today? You are maintaining your weight quite well. You do look a bit tired but that is to be expected."

"The last 3 months of the pregnancy can be very tiring. You should take a nap every day. Go for walks when weather permits. Continue to eat as well as you can and avoid stress."

"Hmm, your blood pressure is a bit high today. And your heart is beating very fast. Are you sure everything is going well?" The doctor turned to look at Nellie Mae because she had not responded to any of his comments.

Nellie Mae burst into tears. "Oh, Doctor. I have had some terrible news. I don't even know what to do now. I need to tell you that my best friend...I mean my husband isn't coming home to me! I don't know what I am going to do now."

The doctor looked very surprised. "What? What do you mean he isn't coming home? Did something happen to him? Please sit down and tell me what is going on."

The doctor helped her to a chair. "Take a deep breath, now let it out. And another deep breath. Now, Mrs. Symthe, tell me what is wrong." the doctor asked as he checked her pulse again.

Nellie Mae covered her face with her hands. "I don't know what to say or how to explain it. He just...he..." Nellie Mae burst into tears again. "I can't keep the baby now. I have no where to go and no one to turn to."

The doctor quietly asked. "But, what about your friend who always comes with you to the appointments? Can't she help you? Where is she today, by the way?"

Nellie Mae continued to sob. "She,...she...she couldn't come. She is going home to be with her parents. So I can't count on her help. I don't want to ask her parents either."

The doctor patted Nellie Mae's hand. "Take another deep breath and try to calm down. You must think of the baby now. Let's talk about options, shall we? Are you sure your husband isn't coming home? Was there a quarrel or misunderstanding? Sometimes men get very nervous when the pregnancy is getting close to the end. Maybe he will change his mind, dear."

"No, I don't think he will accept the baby now. I've thought about it for a long time. I just don't think he will be happy. I mean, **I don't think he was very happy about the pregnancy.** I think I need to be concerned about what is best for the baby now. So, what options do I have at this point, Doctor?"

The doctor responded "Well, I need to check it all out but normally you can sign a document that you are giving the baby up for adoption. The hospital has someone who works with the orphanage and a baby. Well, a baby could probably be placed right away with a family. If not, the baby would be raised in the orphanage until adopted or stay until the age of 18. It's a big decision to make and one that you need to be sure about. You will have until the delivery of the baby to sign the document."

"An orphanage? Oh my, I didn't think the baby would go there! I thought a family would be available to take the baby immediately after the birth! I'm not sure I like the idea of an orphanage. I guess I do have a lot of thinking to do now." Nellie

Mae said. She burst into tears once again as the thought of giving her baby away overwhelmed her with sadness.

"If you are sure you want to give up the baby as soon as you give birth, you can sign the document now. Then the hospital and orphanage can be looking for a good family right away. And by the time, the baby comes, the family might be chosen. That way, the baby would be given directly to the family. But, yes, you do have a lot to think about."

The doctor continued. "I want to see you in 4 weeks to check on you and to make sure that your stress level and your blood pressure are lower."

"Yes, of course, Doctor." Nellie Mae said. "I will do a lot of thinking and hopefully I will have made a decision by the next appointment. Thank you for all the help and the information." Nellie Mae got up from the chair and walked out of the office.

The doctor watched her leave. He knew something wasn't quite right. He thought she had not told him everything. He had known ever since Mrs. Smythe came to his office that she wasn't telling the truth.

But he could see that she was very stressed and upset. He wondered if she was married at all. Well, it was none of his business except to take care of her and her baby and keep her as healthy as possible until the delivery.

He hoped she would reconsider and plan to keep her baby. It was obvious that she wanted the child because she did everything he told her to do to make sure this pregnancy was going well.

CHAPTER TWENTY SIX ~

The next 4 weeks went by very quickly. Nellie Mae found herself lost in thoughts every day. She just couldn't make up her mind. What if she told Hank that Bernie had wanted her to keep Bernie's baby and that was why she had the child in their home? No, that probably wouldn't work because Bernie's parents would want to raise Bernie's child themselves. Besides the baby would be too young to have been Bernie's child.

So what if Nellie Mae told Hank the truth? She was carrying the baby for Bernie and Ed and now she wanted to keep the baby herself? But what if Hank didn't believe how the pregnancy came about. What if he left her and the baby? Oh, what was she going to do?

She had less than 2 months to figure it out. She didn't know what was going to happen to the baby or to her for that matter. And, she hadn't heard from Hank in several weeks. Was he still alive? Would she be in the same situation that Bernie had been?

When Nellie Mae had cleaned out Bernie's unit, she took all the food and other items that she might need, including the ration stamps. She also found the baby clothing that Bernie had made so she took it all as well.

If she decided to give up the baby, she would give all the clothing to the adoptive parents. At least the baby would have a few things from someone who had wanted a baby so much.

In the meantime, she wanted to stay inside her home as much as possible. She didn't want anyone to figure out that she was pregnant. She was sure with all the canned jars of fruit and vegetables that she and Bernie had put up all summer that she would do just fine for the rest of the winter before she had the baby.

CHAPTER TWENTY SEVEN ~

In spite of staying inside, Nellie Mae still had a few visits from the Chaplain and a couple of other wives who had known Bernie. The women stopped by to check on Nellie Mae. She pretended that she was sick with a bad cold. She asked them to take some of the ration stamps and get her some groceries to cook. A couple of the wives even brought her homemade soup and some casseroles, so she had some good meals to eat for a few days.

When four weeks had gone by, Nellie Mae took the bus again for the doctor appointment. She hoped the doctor wouldn't ask too many questions. She still didn't know what the best decision would be for the baby.

"Hello, Mrs. Smythe. How are you feeling today?" the doctor asked as he walked into the examination room. "Let's see how much weight you have gained and then check your heart and your blood pressure, shall we?"

After she got off the scale, the doctor looked at her and said "Well, the weight gain is just right. Your heart sounds very good and your blood pressure is just slightly elevated. That's all good news."

"But how are you feeling emotionally today? Have you made a decision about what to do about the baby?" The doctor looked at Nellie Mae to see if she had any reaction to his questions.

"Do you still think you want to give the baby up for adoption? Or has your husband come around and made amends for his previous decision not to be with you? I do have some new information for you if you are still thinking of adoption."

"What news is that, Doctor?" Nellie Mae asked. She felt her heart beating very fast and she took a deep breath as she sat down in the chair. "What can you tell me?"

"First, what about your husband, dear?" The doctor asked "Has anything changed about that?"

Nellie Mae looked down at her hands folded in her lap. "No, not really, doctor. I still don't think he is going to accept this baby. I don't even know if he is going to forgive me for being pregnant. So, what is the new information you mentioned?"

The doctor smiled and said "Well, the hospital and orphanage work together as I told you during our last visit. I told them there was a possibility of a newborn coming in the next few weeks. They said they have two families who are looking for a baby."

"One family lives in this area on a farm. They have wanted a child for years but couldn't conceive. They really want a son but would be willing to take a girl."

"The other family lives in a town not too far from here. It's North River, have you heard of it? It's not too far away. They have a son but want to have more children. They adopted their son about 2 years ago so they are eager to have another little one to grow up with their son."

"Both the families have been checked out and passed with flying colors. Either family would be a great choice. All you have to do is decide if you want the baby to be placed and you can even pick the family."

Nellie Mae kept her surprise to herself. It couldn't be the family from North River. That was near where she and Bernie had lived. She couldn't bear the idea of seeing a small child that she recognized walking around the town. And what if the baby looked like her? Wouldn't someone be suspicious about that?

So that left the farm family. That might not be so bad. Growing up on a farm, fresh air and the country sounded like a great place to be raised in and a good childhood too. But, yes, she had to make the decision.

She looked at the doctor. "I think that IF I go ahead with the adoption, I would chose the family on the farm. They don't have any children so I am sure they would love my child very much. But I still don't know if I want to give the baby up. I guess I need to keep thinking about it. I promise I will try to make a decision before much longer. Would that be alright, doctor?" Nellie Mae asked.

The doctor responded with a smile. "Of course, it will be fine. I will tell the hospital and orphanage that you decided the farm couple would be your choice IF you go ahead with adoption. So let's schedule your next appointment for 4 weeks from now. After that, I want to see you every week until delivery."

Nellie Mae agreed and said her goodbyes. As she walked to the bus stop, she looked in some of the store windows. She saw a beautiful baby blanket and on an impulse, she went into the store and purchased it. She decided if she gave up the baby, she wanted the baby to have a warm blanket. She might even embroider something on the blanket so she could feel closer to the baby.

CHAPTER TWENTY EIGHT ~

The next few days went by even more quickly. The weather was cold and it had started to snow. Nellie Mae kept a pile of wood on her porch for easy access during the cold days and nights. She wore her heavy sweater and kept a quilt by her side most of the time. When she made a meal, she tried to make food that took a long time to cook to keep the kitchen warmer.

She fixed a fresh pot of cinnamon spice tea and poured herself a cup...

******

She could smell the cinnamon spice in the hot tea as she held the old china cup in her hands. It was so pleasant to sit quietly and daydream. She was aware of the sound of the crackling logs in the fireplace and she felt herself drifting away....

*****

When she realized she had started to drift off again. She opened her eyes to see her husband, Hank, talking to her. He had a frown on his face.

"Wait, Hank. Please…please let me explain. I have to start from the beginning. I'm going to tell you everything. And all of it is the truth. I'm so sorry to disappoint you and I just pray that you will listen to it all. And then, I hope…I hope and pray that you will understand why this happened to me…to us actually. I still haven't figured out what to do and I will tell you the options that are available."

Hank looked at her with sadness in his eyes. He crossed his arms and sat on the couch. "All right, go ahead. I'm listening. I will try not to interrupt you while you are explaining. I can't believe that you would actually betray our wedding vows so I guess I need to take a breath or two and just listen. Please go ahead."

Nellie Mae said a silent prayer to help her get through the explanation. "Oh please, God. Please let Hank listen and understand the dilemma I was in. Maybe I did make the wrong choice by doing this but I was so worried about Bernie that I put her needs ahead of what I knew was right."

Nellie Mae spent several minutes telling Hank the story. When she was finished, she looked at his face.

He looked sad and he had tears in his eyes. He got up from the couch and put his coat on. He started for the door.

"Oh no, Hank. Please don't leave You can ask me any questions you need to know. I've told you the truth. It all really happened that way. I never saw Bernie's brother- in-law. I don't even know his name. And he never knew about me. As far as he knew, Bernie was trying to get pregnant herself. And now that Bernie and Ed are both gone, I doubt the brother-in-law will ever tell anyone. He will probably think she lost the baby."

"Please don't leave me. I'll give the baby up for adoption if that is what it will take for you to stay with me. I'll spend the rest of my life making this up to you. Please, I'm begging you, Hank!" Nellie Mae put her head in her hands and cried.

"I'm just going out to get more wood, Nellie Mae. I need to think about all of this. It sounds very strange but in a way, I can understand why you thought you had to go through with it."

"But I need some time. You've had several months to get used to the idea but I've only had a couple of hours. I want to go out and go for a walk and try to clear my head. I'll bring in some more wood after the walk. You can sit by the fire and rest while I am gone." Hank said with a sad smile.

Nellie Mae breathed a sigh of relief. "Oh, Hank. I hope you can forgive me. I wish I had stuck with my original thoughts and just told Bernie no. But I saw her face every day and her spirit was gone." Nellie Mae continued. "I don't know why I did it except she looked so lost that I couldn't bear to refuse her."

Hank opened the door. "I understand that part, Nellie Mae. But please just let me think about all of this for a little while. I'll bring the wood in when I get back from my walk."

With that, Hank shut the door and started down the sidewalk Nellie Mae peeked out the window. The snow was really coming down now. The sidewalk was already covered over with snow. Hank would probably have to shovel it again before morning.

Nellie Mae went into the kitchen and turned the beef stew down. She added a few more cut up vegetables because she was sure that Hank would be hungry after his walk. She mixed up a batch of biscuits to pop into the oven when he returned

She settled back in her rocking chair and wrapped the quilt around her.. She would be praying and counting the minutes until Hank opened the door again.

Hank did return about an hour later. He brought in more wood for the fire. They had dinner with very little conversation. Both of them were lost in their own thoughts Hank told Nellie Mae he was going to shovel the walk again before bed.

He went outside and stayed out for a very long time. When he came back inside, Nellie Mae had fallen asleep in her rocking chair. He woke her up and helped her to bed. She hardly knew he was there at all.

He went back to the living room and stared into the fire for hours. Then he put more wood on the fire and wrapped himself in the quilt and laid down on the couch. This sure wasn't the way he thought he would be spending his first night home.

He fell asleep as he started going over everything Nellie Mae had told him that afternoon. While it sounded so strange, it still sounded just like Nellie Mae. He knew the bond between Bernie and Nellie Mae had been very strong. He could believe that Nellie Mae would decide she had to help her dearest friend even at the sake of ignoring her own better judgment.

But how did he feel about the baby? Could he accept the child as his own? Could he even be a good father to the baby? Would he see Bernie in the baby's face? That might help him accept the baby. But what if the baby looked like the brother-in-law...a stranger? A constant reminder of how the baby came to be in his life? Could he ever get past the betrayal of their wedding vows?

And if they ever had children of their own, could he still love this baby in the same way he would love his own flesh and blood? As he lay there, pondering all the questions, he fell asleep.

CHAPTER TWENTY NINE ~

The next few days were long ones for both Hank and Nellie Mae. They were polite to each other but they didn't look at each other very much. Both of them were so sad and it showed. They ate their meals together and did their chores too but mostly with just a few words.

Hank always complimented Nellie Mae on the food she prepared. He put on a little weight in spite of all the outside work he was doing. Truth be told, he used the outside work as an excuse to stay away from her and to think. He was still sleeping on the couch every night too.

Nellie Mae was really worried about their marriage. Hank was polite but he wasn't being very friendly. She didn't know what else she could do. She decided to tell Hank that she was going to sign the adoption document when she went to the doctor the next time. The appointment was in a week. Hank had said he would have to go back on duty a few days later.

He reported to his base commander and learned that his unit was being reassigned. Because of the number of injured men in the recent battle, the unit was going to be kept at the home base to help train new recruits. Hank would be given a new position and a promotion for his valor while he was overseas.

Hank was relieved in a way because his unit would be safer in the US than back in Europe. He was going to make sure that all the new recruits were trained properly and thoroughly. He didn't want any more men to be lost in the battlefield. He couldn't wait to tell Nellie Mae the news when she got home from the doctor.

Nellie Mae had gone to the appointment alone. She considered asking Hank if he wanted to go too. But then she would have to explain to the doctor why she had used a false name. She was tired of having to explain her decisions to everyone and just wanted to get through the rest of the pregnancy and then decide what to do with the baby.

The appointment went well. As usual the doctor was pleased with her weight and her heart rate and all the other things he checked. He noted that her blood pressure was a little bit lower. She seems more at ease although she wasn't talking much. He wondered if he should ask about the adoption decision. She didn't seem very interested in talking so he just let the subject go. There was still time. He scheduled her next appointment for the following week. He was sure she wouldn't deliver before that but he wanted to check her emotional state again. Stress could bring on early labor and he was concerned.

Nellie got on the bus to go back to the base. She wondered what Hank's mood would be like when she got home again. She hoped he had the actual date he had to leave. She wanted to fix him as many of his favorite meals as possible before he had to go away again.

She was going to miss him. Not that he was very talkative or affectionate but it was comforting to have him in the house. She felt safer when he was there. And being closer to the end of the pregnancy, she really liked having someone in the house who knew her condition.

She hadn't figured out what to do when the labor pains started. How in the world would she get to the hospital? Maybe she needed to talk to the doctor about a home delivery after all.

By the time Nellie Mae got home. Hank had shoveled the walk and brought more wood up on the porch. He had a fire going in the fireplace. And she could even smell the cinnamon spice tea . He came out of the kitchen with mugs of tea and a plate of cookies she had made the day before.

"Sit down, Nellie Mae. Get warm by the fire. I made some tea and here are some cookies for us to eat. I have some things to tell you. And I want to hear about the doctor appointment. How did it go today? Is everything going the way it should?" Hank asked with a small smile.

Nellie Mae looked a bit surprised at his invitation. "Thank you ,Hank. That smells so good. It's really cold outside and I got chilled walking from the bus stop. Yes, the appointment went well. The doctor was pleased with my weight and all the other factors. He said I should come back in next week."

"He doesn't think I am ready to deliver for at least another 6 weeks. He said first babies are often late in coming any way. I didn't discuss the adoption today but I do know the family that I selected that lives on a farm is interested. They do still want the baby. I guess you and I have to talk about that."

Nellie took a sip of the hot tea and then looked at Hank. He appeared to be lost in thought.

Nellie Mae continued. "So what about you? Did you find out the date you have to leave? How much time do we have left? I have really liked having you home and knowing that you are safe here. But I realize you have a job to do and a duty to fulfill. You will have to make a list of the dinners you want me to make for you before you have to go again."

"No, I am not going to make a list of dinners. I don't have to do that." Hank said.

Nellie Mae felt some tears welling up in her eyes. Was Hank saying that he was leaving her? "What ever do you mean, Hank? I don't understand. I just want to do something nice for you before you go away again."

Hank started laughing. "Oh, Honey, I have great news! Our unit isn't going back overseas at all. We are being reassigned. I'm getting a promotion and a new job assignment training new recruits right here on the base. I don't have to leave you at all or the baby. Isn't that wonderful?"

Nellie Mae's eyes got very big. "Are you saying that you are not leaving me? I mean that you want to stay married to me after all I have done to us? I can't believe it. You are forgiving me? Please, Hank, please tell me what is going on."

Hank stood up and walked over to Nellie Mae's chair. He pulled her up and wrapped his arms around her. "Yes, Nellie Mae. I am staying with you in our marriage. I've thought about it quite a bit."

"I don't entirely agree with the choice you made to carry a baby for Bernie. But I do understand why you did it. I think I am prepared to take care of the baby and I will try to love it as much as I can. I can't say that I won't remember how the baby came to be but I will do everything in my power to love the baby just as much as I would if it were my own child. And besides, the baby is half you so I can love it for that."

With that, Nellie Mae hugged Hank back and said a little prayer of thanks.

The couple had a lovely evening. When it was time for bed, Nellie Mae went ahead and got ready. Hank suggested she take a warm bath before bed so she would be warm and relaxed and comfortable. When she came out of the bathroom, there were candles in the bedroom and the bed was turned down. She walked quietly into the room.

Hank was waiting there for her in the flickering candlelight. He walked over to her and pulled her to him in a gentle hug. "I just have one thing to ask you, Nellie Mae." Hank said softly. "Is it safe for us to be together tonight? By that, I mean I won't hurt you because you are pregnant, will I?"

Nellie Mae smiled back. "No, you won't hurt me. I've missed your touch and your love. I think we can manage to make love without bothering the baby at all."

After her response, Hank helped her out of her robe and her nightgown. He looked at her body in the candlelight and smiled. "Oh, my dearest darling, you are the most beautiful thing I have ever seen."

"Your skin feels like silk under my hands. You smell like the most fragrant rose and you make me forget everything. It's been such a long time since we have been together like this. Come to bed, my sweetheart and let me make you feel how much I love you."

The couple got into bed and spent several moments enjoying each other's body. They got lost in the miracle of their love and when they were completely satisfied, they fell asleep in each others arms. It was the best night of sleep that either of them had experienced in a very, very long time.

CHAPTER THIRTY ~

The next day neither of them could keep their hands off each other. They hugged and kissed and smiled and laughed throughout the entire day.

Hank asked Nellie Mae about what they needed for the baby. She showed him all the things that Bernie had made and the baby blanket that Nellie Mae had embroidered with tiny animals. She discussed that they would need a baby bed or a cradle and some cotton fabric to make diapers. She said since they were keeping the baby that she wanted to breastfeed the baby to feel a special bond with the infant.

Hank smiled. He said he had an idea and it was going to be a secret. No matter how much Nellie Mae tried to guess, he wouldn't give her any clues. Then Hank asked if Nellie Mae wanted him to go to the doctor with her for the next visit.

Nellie Mae thought it over and said "Yes, I would. I want to tell the doctor the truth about this whole situation and if you are positive you want us to keep the baby, I want to tell him that as well."

"I'm positive that I have made up my mind but I will let you know for sure how I feel when the child is here." Hank cautioned.

As the days went by, Hank was often away for long hours. He had his new duties to handle. He seemed to be enjoying the job and often had stories to share about his day when he got home for dinner.

Nellie Mae continued to work on the baby's layette and fussed over making a place for the baby to sleep. And she cooked as many meals as she could in advance just in case her labor started earlier than expected.

Soon the doctor visit was on the schedule. Hank and Nellie Mae took the bus to town. As they walked into the doctor's office, they each held hands. Nellie Mae said a little prayer for courage as they went into the examination room. The doctor walked in reading the chart. As he looked up at Nellie Mae, he became aware that a man was also in the room. "This must be your husband, Mrs. Smythe?" he asked with a smile.

"Mrs. Smythe? You must have the wrong chart, doctor. This is my wife, Nellie Mae Hamilton. I'm Captain Harold Hamilton. I recently returned from overseas. Nellie Mae has told me of the unusual circumstances of this pregnancy and I am supporting her decision." Hank said as he shook the doctor's hand.

"I...I must be mistaken then, Captain. I was sure your wife introduced herself as Mrs. Smythe." The doctor to take a long look at Nellie Mae. "So what's the story, Mrs.. Uh....Hamilton?"

Nellie Mae stammered. "I'm so sorry that I lied to you, Doctor. I can explain everything now that I've talked to my husband." Nellie Mae once again told the long and involved story of how she became pregnant and why she made that decision. When she was finished, she looked at Hank and at the doctor.

"Well, that certainly was an unusual way to get pregnant but I guess it worked out. I've never heard of doing it that way. Hmmm, interesting! I have a lot of patients who haven't been able to conceive. Imagine that… a turkey baster! Hmmmm I wonder if this would work for them?…Well, never mind about that now." the doctor said.

"Now, let's talk about your pregnancy and give you a more thorough examination this time. I want to try to determine when you might be ready for delivery." the doctor continued.

After the exam, the doctor talked to both Hank and Nellie Mae about what to expect in the next few weeks. He explained about labor pains and how they might feel. He told Nellie Mae that if she tried to relax with the pains, it would go much easier for her. He told her to call him as soon as the labor pains felt strong and were about 8 minutes apart. He assured both Hank and Nellie Mae that he had a car and he could get to their home if necessary. As they left, he scheduled another visit in two weeks in case she had not delivered by then.

Hank and Nellie Mae had a lot to talk about on the way home. Hank was a bit surprised that Nellie Mae and Bernie had lied to the doctor. But in thinking it over, he realized why they did.

Hank was determined to be there for Nellie Mae. He had given a lot of thought to accepting this baby and he was almost positive that he could do it. He loved Nellie Mae with all his heart and he had to be there for her. It was the right thing to do.

CHAPTER THIRTY ONE ~

As the next few days went by, Hank and Nellie Mae continued to prepare for the baby. Hank's big secret was that he had decided to make a cradle. He worked on it at the base wood shop whenever he had time. But finally he needed to bring it inside the house to finish the detailing.

Nellie Mae was taking a nap in the bedroom as Hank worked on the final finishing touches. When she woke up, she walked into the living room and stopped. Her mouth fell open. She couldn't speak for a few moments. And then the tears started to fall.

She looked at Hank and said. "I can't believe you did this for me and for the baby. It's the most loving and beautiful thing you have ever done for me. I love you so much. And even though you said you would stay with me and be a father to this child, I didn't think you really meant it. But this makes me feel so much better and so optimistic that we can be a family. Thank you so much." Nellie Mae walked over to Hank and put her arms around him as she quietly continued to cry.

Finally, when she had stopped crying, Hank walked her over to her rocking chair.

He asked "Where should we put the cradle? Do you want it out here near the fireplace where it is warm or do you need it in the bedroom? I'll put it where ever you think best. I don't know how to be a father yet but I want to learn. Please help me learn, my darling. I do want to be a good father and I will pray for guidance and wisdom but I will still need your help too. So will you teach me, Nellie Mae?"

"Of course, I will. I have to learn to be a mother too. I know a bit about taking care of children but I have never had a newborn to care for. We can learn together. I'm really so grateful that we have the opportunity to go through this together, Hank." Nellie Mae answered.

Nellie Mae continued. "It's just you and I for now. When the baby is older, we can take it back home for a visit. By then it won't be so strange that we have a baby."

Hank agreed. He placed the cradle close to the fireplace where it would be accessible during the day. At night, they might have to figure something else out but probably the warmest place would still be by the fireplace. He thought about putting some sort of wheels on the cradle so it could easily be moved but still rock. Maybe he should build a frame for the cradle to be suspended from to make it easier for Nellie Mae to move it if necessary when he wasn't home.

Hank silently prayed he could be a good father and do this and find love for this child that was not his own. It would be half Nellie Mae's so he thought he could think of that and find some love for the coming baby. At least, he hoped he could. "God, please help me do this." Hank prayed.

CHAPTER THIRTY TWO ~

At the next doctor appointment, Nellie Mae was told that the birth was not far off. The doctor told her again what the signs of active labor would be. He told both Hank and Nellie Mae to be sure to stay close to home so they would have time to get to the hospital when it was necessary. The couple looked a bit apprehensive but they knew they could do it together.

About two nights later, Nellie Mae woke up. She was lying on her stomach which she had never been able to do since early in her pregnancy. She was confused and wondered where she was and what was happening.

She got up to use the bathroom and felt a strange sensation of pulsing as liquid went down her legs. She then realized her water must have broken. She grabbed an old towel to wipe up the puddle as she felt more liquid coming out of her body. She stuck the towel between her legs and walked back into the bedroom.

"Hank, Hank, wake up! I think I have started labor. I haven't felt any pains yet but…oh wait…oh my! I think I just had a labor pain! Get up so we can time the contractions. Doctor said we needed to call him and head to the hospital when the pains are about 8 minutes apart."

"Let's...oh my…there's another one! They aren't too painful but they definitely are different from anything I have felt before. Do you have your pocket watch? Here goes another one. Those are very close together, aren't they? Do you think something is wrong?" Nellie Mae said with a frightened sound in her voice.

Hank got up and put his arms around Nellie Mae. "Let's go into the living room. I'll build up the fire and you can sit in your rocker. Here, wrap this quilt around you so you don't get chilled, Honey."

Hank helped Nellie Mae into the living room and settled her in the rocking chair. He got out his pocket watch and asked her to tell him when she had the next contraction. It was about 6 minutes when she felt another one. They kept track for a few more minutes and realized the contractions were coming fairly regularly every 6 or 7 minutes.

Hank told Nellie Mae he thought they should go to the hospital. But how were they going to get there? The buses didn't run at night. They didn't have a car either. The only thing they could do was call the doctor for help. Hank put on his coat and said he was walking to the guard shack to see if he could get a car from the base before he called the doctor. He would come back as soon as he found out.

It seemed like forever before he returned. Nellie Mae had more contractions while he was gone. They were getting stronger and closer. Nellie Mae had decided to get dressed so she would be ready to go.

Hank came through the door and said "I ran into the Chaplain at the church. He was working on his next sermon. He asked if something was wrong so I told him you needed to go to the hospital. He said he would get a car and drive us. Put on your coat and bring the quilt so you stay warm. Should I bring the little suitcase you packed for the hospital stay too?"

Nellie Mae looked confused and a bit frightened. She didn't know what was going to happen when the time for having this baby arrived. It seems like the months had gone by way too quickly. She wasn't sure she was ready for this new experience! She had expected Bernie to be with her when this baby was born. She blinked back some tears and got up.

"Yes, dear. The suitcase is under the bed on my side. I already put in a warm gown for the baby and a sweater and hat with the blanket I embroidered. I'll get my coat and hat on while you bank the fire and close up the house."

They both heard the sound of a car outside. It was time to go. They walked outside and the Chaplain came to take the suitcase. He apologized that all he could borrow was a Jeep but he suggested they wrap up in blankets and try to stay covered. He drove to the hospital in the city as quickly as he could. As he stopped at the front door, he asked "Do you want me to stay? Might I be of some comfort to you both?"

Nellie Mae was having another contraction and couldn't even respond. Hank thought for a moment and said "Yes, Chaplain. I would like you to be here with us. I think we need to explain what has been going on so this won't come as a shock to you. Perhaps you can help me talk to the Base Commander also after the baby comes. It's a delicate situation for us."

Hank and the chaplain guided Nellie Mae to the front desk. She was admitted and taken away to the maternity ward. Hank was told he should remain in the lobby until someone came for him to bring him up to date on Nellie Mae's progress with the labor and then the birth.

While he waited, he briefly told the chaplain what had been going on. As the story was revealed, the chaplain finally understood why Bernie and Nellie Mae had stayed to themselves so much. And why they had been going into town every few weeks. He assured Hank that their information would be kept confidential.

He also said he would speak with the Base Commander. Perhaps Hank could ask for a transfer or be could be reassigned to another base so their secret would not be discovered or questioned by anyone else on the base if the young couple was concerned about any gossip that might be started when they brought home a baby.

About an hour later, a nurse came to get Hank. She said Nellie Mae also wanted to speak with the chaplain. She took them both to a ward which had several beds in it. Nellie Mae had a curtain around her bed. Both men walked inside the curtained cubicle to talk with Nellie Mae. Hank told her that the chaplain knew the background story.

Nellie Mae started to cry. "I'm so ashamed, Chaplain. I didn't want to do this but I felt I had no other choice but to help my dearest friend, Bernie. And then everything fell apart. She lost her husband, Ed. Then, she didn't want the baby!. She was falling apart before my eyes. I couldn't save her. I feel like this is all my fault. I never should have agreed to it!"

"Oh Chaplain, am I being punished for my sins? Will this baby be born with sin hanging over its head? What can I do to be forgiven? Please tell me."

The Chaplain smiled and took Nellie Mae's hand. "Oh my dear. You haven't done anything with malice in your heart . You haven't really sinned at all. You did the best you could do for your friend, Bernie. You sacrificed so much to help her."

"God still loves you for your decisions. He forgives you for what you did. I'm so sorry it came to that. I know you have strong morals and that this decision tested your spirit and your strength. It might not have been the best solution for Bernie's needs but it certainly was done with the greatest love for her."

"This baby will be loved by you as a remembrance of Bernie. And Hank has told me that he will be by your side all the way . I will be pleased to pray for all of you. And when the time comes, I would be honored to perform the baptism of this baby who was so much wanted by all of you. Now let me say a prayer for you and then I will leave Hank with you for now."

After the prayer, the Chaplain quietly spoke to Hank. He told him that he would be in the fathers waiting room if Hank wanted to talk further. He excused himself and left the ward. As he walked to the waiting room, he said a prayer that this would turn out well. A healthy baby and a loving family would be the best outcome of a serious and delicate situation.

He vowed to speak to the Base Commander and do everything he could to help the young couple and the baby find a new home to start over with no gossipy stories circulating around the base.

Goodness knows Nellie Mae had gone through enough losing her dearest friend and then having to explain her reasoning for betraying her wedding vows to her own husband.

CHAPTER THIRTY THREE ~

The labor pains got stronger and Nellie Mae concentrated on the instructions the nurse gave her. The doctor stopped in to check on her progress and assured her it was all going very well. He said he would be back in a few minutes. He wanted to look at the delivery room and make sure it was all in order for the birth. As he left the ward, he motioned to Hank to step outside the door.

"Hank, I just want to assure you that the birth should go just fine. Nellie Mae is a strong young woman and she wants this baby very much. I know you said you would stand beside her and the baby. I certainly hope you will keep that promise!" the doctor said.

He then added ."I can assure you that I believe Nellie Mae got pregnant with the only intention of helping her friend, Bernie. When they used to come for the examinations, Bernie was always so eager to know what was happening and what she could do to help Nellie Mae have a healthy baby. I thought at the time that it was a bit unusual but now that I know the full story, it all makes sense."

"I'm really sorry that Bernie took her life after she lost her husband. "I can't imagine how difficult that loss has been for Nellie Mae too. But now Nellie Mae is going to be a mother and I hope you can keep your promise and stay true to your resolve. If I can be of assistance to you in any way , I want to be there. Now I am going to examine Nellie Mae again as soon as I check the delivery room. It shouldn't be too long now."

Hank returned to Nellie Mae's cubicle and held her hand. He told her how proud he was of her strength. He told her that he was excited about the baby's birth. He told her he was honestly a bit overwhelmed but he was determined to be the man she could count on.

The doctor came back into the cubicle as Hank stepped out. He quickly checked Nellie Mae and told her it was time. The orderlies wheeled her bed out and headed toward the delivery room.
Hank gave Nellie Mae a kiss as she left the area.

The doctor told Hank to go to the fathers waiting room and that as soon as the birth had been completed that the doctor would come to talk with Hank.

CHAPTER THIRTY FOUR ~

It seemed like Hank had barely gotten settled in the waiting room and spoken to the Chaplain when the doctor walked into the room.

"Well, that was quick!" the doctor said with a smile on his face. "Everything went very well and Nellie Mae is doing just fine. She did such a good job and I think she is very happy."

"But what did she have, Doctor?" Hank quickly asked. "Is it a boy? She was sure it was a boy. Is the baby alright? Everything is good?"

The doctor answered with a chuckle. "Yes, all the fingers and toes are there. The baby weighs 7 lbs, 4 ounces and judging by the noise, the baby is very healthy. And by the way, it's a girl!"

"A girl? What am I going to do with a girl?I mean I don't know much about girls at all! I grew up as an only child. Most of my friends were boys. I thought having a baby boy would not be as difficult because I could teach him to play ball and run and climb and fish and...oh no! This is not what I expected at all!" Hank said to the doctor.

The doctor laughed. "If I know anything about fathers and baby girls, she will have you wrapped around her little finger in no time. Would you like to see her? She should be in the nursery by now. And your wife, Nellie Mae, will be back in the ward in just a few more minutes."

"Is Nellie Mae alright? Is she in pain? Does she know the baby is a girl?" Hank quickly asked the doctor. "I think I should see Nellie Mae first. We have a lot of talking to do since the baby is a girl instead of the boy we planned on." Hank responded.

"Well, yes, you can see Nellie Mae first. I'll have the nurse come get you when she is ready for visitors. Are you sure you don't want to see the baby now while you are waiting for Nellie Mae? Don't you want to see what she looks like, Hank?" the doctor questioned.

"Oh, I guess so. I'm just all confused. I had my heart set with plans for a son. I guess I need to rethink those plans and figure out how I am going to be a good father to a baby girl. Where is the baby again, Doctor?" Hank answered.

"I'll take you straight to the nursery myself so you can see her. She's a beauty in my opinion. I think you will agree. She's very healthy too. She has strong lungs based on how she cried right when she was being born. She was hollering before she was completely out of Nellie Mae. That's an excellent sign of her strength and will." The doctor laughed.

CHAPTER THIRTY FIVE ~

Once Hank arrived at the nursery window, he started looking at all the babies in the bassinets. Soon the nurse brought a pink blanketed bundle up to the window. She moved the blanket away from the baby's face. The baby yawned and then started to cry.

"What's wrong with her, Doctor? Why is she crying? Is she in pain?" Hank quickly asked the doctor.

"No, Hank. She is just fine. She is opening up her lungs and filling her body with oxygen. It's actually good for her to cry right now. She is getting pinker and even more healthy."

"I talked to Nellie Mae before and she wants to nurse the baby. So soon the nurse will take the baby to Nellie Mae and show her how to do that. It might take a little time and some patience but I am sure, with a bit of practice, Nellie Mae and the baby will figure it all out. If not, there is always formula and baby bottles."

"Now, Nellie Mae should be back in the ward. Let's go see her too, Hank." The doctor started to walk towards the maternity ward with Hank hurrying behind him.

The doctor peeked behind the curtain and motioned Hank to come in. Nellie Mae was sleeping. She looked so beautiful and so peaceful that Hank didn't want to wake her. He sat in the chair by her bed and picked up her hand.

She started to stir and Hank quickly squeezed her hand and whispered "Oh my dearest, the baby has come. It's not what we expected or at least, not what I was expecting. I had made all sorts of plans on raising a son. But now, I have to figure out what to do with a baby girl. Are you disappointed it's a girl, my darling?" Hank said to Nellie Mae as she opened her eyes.

"Oh Hank, I'm thrilled we have a baby girl! I can't wait to dress her up in all the little pink outfits that Bernie had made. Bernie secretly wanted a girl too."

Nellie Mae smiled and said "Ed was the one who wanted a son. I guess most men think they can relate better with a boy, don't they? Are you terribly upset that we have a girl, dear?" Nellie Mae asked.

"No, I'm just a bit surprised. So I guess we need to pick out a name for this baby girl. Do you want to name her after Bernie? Or your mother? Or yourself?" Hank said.

"Well, I want to see her first. I did see her right after the birth but I was so sleepy, I can't remember what she looks like. I hope they bring her in soon so I can get acquainted with her. Maybe once I see her, I can think of a name for her. Is that alright with you, Hank? Did you have a name in mind?" Nellie Mae wondered.

"No. No name in mind. I don't care what the name is actually. As long as you like it, I will be ok with whatever you decide. I'm sure you will come up with an appropriate name for your little girl." Hank answered.

"Hank! She's OUR baby girl! I want us both to be in agreement about the name. When I think of one or two names, I'll talk to you about them and we will decide together." Nellie Mae said with a smile.

The nurse came in at that time and told Hank that visiting hours were over. He needed to leave but he could come back the next day. The nurse wanted to get Nellie Mae ready to see the baby and instruct her on how to nurse her.

Hank walked out to the lobby where he found the Chaplain waiting. "Oh, Chaplain, I forgot you were here. I'm sorry I took so long. I guess I am supposed to go home now according to the nurse."

"Well, Hank. Congratulations! I asked the doctor how Nellie Mae was and he said she was just fine. She will be tired tonight but I am sure she is very happy."

"And what about you, Hank? How does it feel to be a father? The father of a beautiful baby girl! I had a chance to see the baby and give her a blessing in the nursery. I hope that was agreeable to you?" the Chaplain asked Hank.

"What? Oh, of course, Chaplain. Of course! I'm sorry…I guess I am still a bit confused. Having a baby girl wasn't what I expected to hear from the doctor. I saw her for a few moments too. She looks healthy and she was crying. Well, she was crying quite a bit. The doctor assured me that she was in good health and that she should be crying to get oxygen in her lungs."

"I guess Nellie Mae is going to try to nurse her later today. I hope that works out because I know Nellie Mae wanted to feel that special bond with the baby." Hank added.

The Chaplain responded. "I'm sure it is going to work out just fine. So, let's get back to the base so I can return the Jeep to the Motor Pool. And I also want to bring the Base Commander up to speed."

"Maybe he will have information on a transfer for you as well. I know you and Nellie Mae would like to start fresh in a new place where people won't question the baby's birth."

"Yes, that's a good idea, Chaplain. Let's go." Hank answered. "I have a lot of plans to follow through with before Nellie Mae brings the baby home."

CHAPTER THIRTY SIX ~

Hank and the Chaplain returned to the base and they both spoke with the Base Commander. He congratulated Hank on the birth.

Then the Base Commander cleared his throat and said "I don't know what this has to do with you or if it has anything to do with you wanting to be transferred, Captain Hamilton."
"
"I got an inquiry from the Navy about Nellie Mae's friend, Bernadette Dawson, a week or so ago. It seems Mrs. Dawson's brother-in-law who is actually her late husbands brother was asking about her death. He called me yesterday. He seemed convinced that Mrs. Dawson was pregnant at the time of her passing. I told him that she wasn't and that investigation clearly indicated that she had taken several pain killers and had drown in her own bathtub. The man didn't seem convinced but he said he would think about it and get back to me. Does that worry you at all?"

"No sir, it doesn't. I expect that Mrs. Dawson was in touch with Ed's family after he died but I don't know about a brother." Hank added "Not to change the subject, but Sir, you were also going to see if there were any transfers available."

The Base Commander responded "Yes, I did check. There are two different options for a transfer and it would be up to you to decide. Let me show you the information."

The Base Commander suggested that Hank discuss it with Nellie Mae too since she would be living on the base with a newborn. Hank promised he would talk to Nellie Mae the next day and report back to the Base Commander. Hank thanked both men for all their assistance and understanding. He walked back to the little house.

He sat on the couch and got lost in thought. "What a difference a few hours make!" Hank reflected. "This is not what I thought was going to happen. What am I going to do now?"

He reread the paperwork on the two different bases he could choose from. He talked to himself as he read. "Just where should we decide to live? One option is in California which is clear across the country. The weather would be great. We would have the ocean and the flowers and the weather to enjoy for sure. But we would be so far away from our families. But maybe that would be a good thing. We can wait to announce the birth of the baby until at least nine months since I returned to the base here."

"The other option is in Texas which isn't as far away but the weather isn't quite as good. I guess I need to talk with Nellie Mae and see what she thinks she wants to do."

The next day Hank took the bus to town and walked to the hospital again. He went directly to Nellie Mae's cubicle in the maternity ward. She was looking at a magazine that a nurse had brought her. She heard Hank when he stepped into the cubicle area.

She smiled at him and said "Well, hello there Papa! How does it feel to be a father? Are you excited? Have you seen her today? She's so beautiful. She did a good job nursing too. We tried every 3 hours during the night and this morning. The nurse even said that the baby will have already gained a few ounces by the time we leave the hospital! Isn't that wonderful?" Nellie Mae's face was glowing.

She was so happy that Hank didn't want to say anything that would take her joy away.

Hank finally said "Um, when I returned to the base yesterday, the Chaplain and I talked to the Base Commander. He has two options on where I...I mean, where WE can be transferred."

"Actually it can happen right away if you think you are up to a move. Let me tell you about each place. Then we need to decide so the Base Commander can put the transfer in the works."

"I can start packing at home while you are recuperating in the hospital. Maybe by the time you are ready to leave, we will have the orders and can go directly to the new place the next week. Do you think you would be strong enough for that, my darling? I'd really like to move as soon as we possibly can."

"Oh my, well I wasn't expecting that to come up so quickly. It would make it easier for us if we don't have to avoid talking about having a baby. So tell me everything. Yes, I think we can manage to move within a week or so. As long as the baby is nursing well and we have diapers and clothes for her, she should be just fine." Nellie Mae answered.

As they talked about the pros and cons of each location, it soon became clear that they both were drawn to the idea of California with the warm weather and the beautiful ocean and many places to visit. So, they decided that Hank would ask for the transfer to be as soon as possible. Nellie Mae had been told she should be able to go home in 3 more days.

"But now, dear, we have something else to discuss." Nellie Mae said.

Hank looked puzzled. "What else is there to talk about?"

Nellie Mae giggled. "We have to name our baby, silly. Have you come up with any names at all?"

Hank looked blank and said "No, actually I haven't. I don't have many girls on my side of the family so I don't have any particular preferences. What have you thought of, darling?" Hank answered.

Nellie Mae sat up straight and folded her hands in her lap. "Well...actually I have come up with an idea. I don't want to name her after me or Bernie."

"But I did think of a name that might work out. How about Rosalyn Marie? We could call her Rosie for short. And Marie is a close name to my mother, Mary. What do you think, Hank? Do you like it?"

"I do! I even think there was a Marie in my family. I think my parents would be pleased. Yes, I like it. It's a very pretty name. So Rosalyn Marie it is!" Hank said with a smile.

Hank and Nellie Mae walked slowly down to the nursery and looked at their baby girl, Rosalyn Marie. She was sleeping peacefully and looks like a little pink angel lying in her bassinet.

Nellie Mae thought to herself. "I can't believe how happy I am at this moment."

Hank thought "Can I do this? Can I be a father to this child who is not of my blood? Can I fall in love with Rosalyn Marie and love her as much as I love her mother, Nellie Mae? Please God, help me. I don't really feel any connection to the baby yet. I hope that will come with time. But what if it doesn't? How could I ever expect Nellie Mae to understand that I might not love this baby as much as she wants me to love it?" .

CHAPTER THIRTY SEVEN ~

Hank was kept busy for the next few days packing up their possessions and cleaning the little housing unit on the base. Nellie Mae came home with little Rosalyn Marie for two days before they had to leave for their new location. Fortunately they were going to travel by train and would have a sleeping compartment. Rosalyn Marie was a good baby and hardly made a peep unless she was hungry or wet. That made the transition into being parents much easier for all of them.

When they arrived at their destination in California. They found that the new Base Commander had sent a car for them. He even made arrangements for their possessions to be placed inside the new housing. The appliances had been turned on as well as the utilities. They were pleasantly surprised to find the housing was newly constructed and very neat and clean. All they had to do was to unpack their personal possessions and place them where they wanted them to go. This was turning into a good move.

Nellie Mae and Hank were both looking forward to starting over fresh. They got settled into the house that evening. They got Rosalyn Marie down for a few hours. Hank made a brief trip to the PX for some basics so Nellie Mae made a quick supper of scrambled eggs and bacon with hot coffee. It tasted so good after eating on the train for a couple of days.

Nellie Mae was clearly very tired. Hank encouraged her to go to bed early that night and get as much sleep as she could before Rosalyn Marie needed to nurse again. Nellie Mae took him up on his offer and after a hot bath, she fell asleep right after she turned the bed covers down.

Hank checked on her and then he looked in Rosalyn Marie's cradle. She was sleeping so sweetly. She really was a beautiful baby and very well behaved too. He wondered how long it would be before she slept all night. Waking up every 3 or 4 hours disrupted everyone's sleep but Hank knew it was only for a short time. There was something very beautiful about watching Nellie Mae nurse the baby that filled his heart with joy.

Hank thought again about being a father to a child that wasn't his own. He really had his doubts that he could be a good father. He tried praying every night for help and guidance on doing the right thing.

There was no way that Nellie Mae would ever understand if he didn't treat the baby well. He had to make himself feel close to the baby somehow.

He wished there was a book he could read that would help him feel the way Nellie Mae felt about the baby. He decided he would work on making the biggest effort he could to accomplish that.

CHAPTER THIRTY EIGHT ~

Weeks went by and the baby continued to thrive. Soon she was sleeping all night which helped everyone get a better night's sleep.

Every day Nellie Mae had something new to tell Hank about when he came home. She was glowing with pride over her beautiful baby girl. She had met some other military wives and some of them also had very young children. She was happy to have some other sources of information to go to when she had questions about Rosalyn Marie and her needs.

As the weeks went by, Rosalyn Marie grew quickly. She was eating some cereal and had a taste of fruit a few times a week. She was a happy baby and was already trying to roll over.

Her hair was still sparse and very light. Nellie Mae tried to get the top tuft into a ribbon. As she looked at her, she could see that the hair was very red. In fact, when the sun was shining on her head, she looked like she had a golden red halo. Nellie Mae thought the baby looked adorable. She dressed her up in a cute outfit and waited for Hank to come home.

When Hank walked into the house, he headed straight for the kitchen. He was so hungry after a long and busy day working outside. Nellie Mae was at the stove and turned when she heard him come in. She gave him a quick hug and kiss.

"Take a look at our beautiful baby girl, Hank!" Nellie Mae said laughing. "Look at the little curl I managed to get into a ribbon on top of her head. Isn't she just the best looking baby you have every seen?"

Hank turned with a smile and then he stared and then he said "Oh no! She's got red hair! Oh no, what are people going to think? What are we going to do? This is too much!"

"What in the world is wrong with you, Hank? Why does red hair bother you so much? It's just hair and it makes her blue eyes look so pretty." Nellie Mae questioned.

"It's RED!, Nellie Mae. RED!!!! We both have dark brown hair. How will we ever explain it? Did her father have red hair?" Hank demanded.

Nellie Mae's voice trembled as she answered …"I never SAW her father, Hank. I've told you that before. I told you how he stayed out in the living room and he gave his specimen to Bernie. He thought she was trying to get pregnant, remember?" Nellie Mae answered quickly. "What difference does it make now? We have a baby girl and she's ours, that is all that matters, isn it, Hank?"

Hank retorted. "Well, she's YOURS! She's really not mine at all. So that's why I am upset with this entire situation."

Nellie Mae was heartbroken. Was Hank saying that he didn't love Rosalyn Marie? Was she going to be known as the redheaded stepchild. The child that no one wanted or loved? How could that be?

Nellie Mae vowed that she would love her baby girl with all her heart. And if Hank couldn't accept her as his daughter and love her just as much as if she were his own, then... Well, then Nellie Mae might have to rethink what she was going to do.

But in the meantime, Nellie Mae got supper on the table, fed Rosalyn Marie and put the baby to bed. Then she silently sat in the living room and did some embroidery of some of Rosalyn Marie's little clothes. There was very little conversation between the couple that evening.

After a few days, Hank did make an effort to spent more of his time with Rosalyn Marie. Sometimes it seemed like Nellie Mae purposely asked him to hold Rosalyn Marie or get something for the baby. It seemed to help him get over some of his attitude towards Rosalyn Marie.

As she grew bigger and started to crawl and then toddle around the house, he even laughed when she made funny faces or did something cute. She seemed especially drawn to him. She was always babbling at him about something. And even when he didn't understand what she was trying to say; he could feel his heart melting. Maybe he could find a way to accept her.

One day he got a phone call from the Chaplain from the original base they had moved from. The Chaplain told Hank that a man had come to look for his sister-in-law. He was looking for Bernie Dawson!

The Chaplain repeated the information about what had happened to Bernie and Ed to the man. He even showed the man the death certificates on file.. The man wanted to know if there was a baby.

When the Chaplain said no, the man kept questioning him saying that Bernie had told him there was a pregnancy. The Chaplain said the man didn't look like Ed Dawson or Bernie. And the man had red hair! But more than that, he even told the Chaplain that he wasn't going to give up until he found the baby.

Hank was very frightened. Was that red headed man the father of Rosalyn Marie? Would he be visiting Bernie's parents in their home town asking questions about a baby? How could Hank and Nellie Mae go back home to see her parents with a red headed child? This could change everything!

CHAPTER THIRTY NINE ~

Hank was letting this information eat him up. He was irritable and snapped at Nellie Mae almost every day. She kept asking him if something was wrong at work. Of course, he denied everything. Nellie Mae was not as happy as she normally was. Even Rosalyn Marie's mood had changed. She cried more often and had trouble eating and sleeping. No one was doing well at all. And something had to be done.

One evening after Nellie Mae put Rosalyn Marie to bed, she walked into the living room and turned off the radio. She took the newspaper away from Hank's hand and told him they had to talk.

"I don't know what is wrong with you, Hank, but we have to figure it out. You seldom smile, or even talk to me unless you are trying to pick a fight. You don't pay any attention to Rosalyn Marie and she can feel the rejection. Just what is your problem?" Nellie Mae said with a break in her voice.

Nellie Mae continued "Don't you love me any more? You never call me darling or dearest like you always have before. You don't even talk about work. So just what is going on?"

Hank looked at her with sadness in his eyes. "I'm sorry, Nellie Mae. I should have told you several weeks ago about what has happened. I just thought I could fix it and you would never have to know."

Hank then told her the whole story that the Chaplain had told him about the redheaded man. "I'm worried about what that man may do. If he goes to your home town and speaks with Bernie's parents, they will probably tell him there was no baby. But since he's Ed's brother and he knows Ed is also dead, he might want to take the baby because it is half his child. If we go back there and people see that we have a red-headed child, they are going to put two and two together and it won't turn out well at all."

Nellie Mae answered. "So, what do we do now? Do we try to get another base assignment? Somewhere far enough away that we can't go home?"Do you think you can get past this news?"

"What do you need to do, Hank? I don't want to lose our family. I love you just as much, if not more than I did when we got married. I want you in Rosalyn Marie's life too. Can we try again, please?" Nellie Mae begged her husband.

Hank agreed that they should try to work things out. He promised not to keep any secrets from her any more. He also said he would make a big effort to change his attitude and become the man that he was before. And he did.

Before long, the little family was happier again. Rosalyn Marie was starting to put words together. She called Hank her Papa and Nellie Mae was Mommy. When she tried to refer to her self, she managed to get Rosie out of her mouth so that became her nickname. She got her cheerful and bubbly personality back too.

She loved to play with a little rag doll that Nellie Mae had made for her. She carried the doll she named Annie around with her everywhere…to bed…to the table when she ate…on walks around the base…and anywhere else she went.

After that, time seemed to fly by. Rosie was learning more and was curious about everything. She was constantly asking "why" and "what's that" over and over again. Nellie Mae patiently answered all her questions the best that she could.

When Rosie was two years old, Nellie Mae told her that they had a secret. She whispered in Rosie's ear that she was going to have a baby brother or sister. Rosie was thrilled with the idea of a baby. She talked to Annie about it and she giggled all the time.

A few weeks later, when Rosie was kissing Papa good night. She asked him if he wanted a baby *brudder or sissy.* Of course, Hank had no idea what she was talking about. He looked at Nellie Mae who blushed and quickly took Rosie to her bed to read her a story and to be tucked under the covers with Annie.

When Nellie Mae returned to the living room, Hank was waiting with a cup of hot tea. "So, is there something you want to tell me, my darling?" he asked. "I finally figured out what Rosie was trying to say. So is there a baby on the way?"

Nellie Mae smiled. "Yes, there is. I haven't gone to the base doctor yet but I am sure I am pregnant. How do you feel about it? Are you happy to have another baby coming? I hope you are. I hope this will make you feel better about being Rosie's father too. What do you think, Hank?" Nellie Mae asked.

"Well, I have thought about what it would be like to have a child of my own...well, I mean...of our own. I know that Rosie is as much my child as yours but you also know that sometimes I have a problem dealing with the fact that you had another man's child in spite of the reasons. So, yes, I am very happy. How do you feel about a new baby, Nellie Mae?" Hank questioned.

Nellie Mae answered with a big smile. "I'm thrilled too! I wanted Rosie to have a brother or sister or even two. I want us to have a complete family and I think this will turn out well for all of us. I'll get an appointment with the doctor tomorrow and try to figure out when this baby will come."

"Thank goodness, I have all of Rosie's baby things. Maybe it will be another girl and I won't have to buy too much more. But if it is a boy, it will be a thrill to have him. I know you would love to have a son at last too!"

"Of course, I would. I always wanted a son. I hope this will help me bond even more with Rosie too. I can't even imagine having two little ones in our home though. It should get much more noisy in a few months."

"Where are we going to put another child anyway?" Hank smiled "I wonder if we can be eligible for larger housing accommodations with a new baby on the way. I'll check into that once the doctor has confirmed you are pregnant."

Nellie Mae answered. "It sounds like we will be very busy for the next few months, darling."

CHAPTER FORTY ~

The pregnancy was confirmed and the doctor thought the baby would arrive around the first week of November. Hank checked with Housing and found out there would be a 3 bedroom unit available shortly after the first of the year. It sounded like things were falling into place once again.

Nellie Mae took a nap every afternoon when Rosie took hers. Nellie Mae took Rosie for a walk every day that the weather permitted too. She had a good appetite and ate quite well. The pregnancy was not too difficult once she got over the usual morning sickness. All in all, the family was doing very well.

Hank made a big effort to spend plenty of time with Rosie. He took her for walks in the evening and on his days off. He read her stories and tried to listen to her babbling about her baby doll, Annie. He even started making a doll cradle for Rosie's big Christmas gift as Nellie Mae worked on doll clothes for Annie.

As for Nellie Mae, she was pleased and relieved to watch Hank getting closer to Rosie. It was still a concern because she caught him looking oddly at Rosie from time to time. She hoped when the new baby came that he would relax into being a good father to both children. She was worried that he would think of the new baby as his child more than Rosie was.

One morning Nellie Mae decided to clean out the bedroom closet because she was looking for the baby clothes she had stored when Rosie was a baby. She wanted to see what basic essentials she needed regardless of whether the new baby was a boy or another girl.

She pulled a kitchen chair into the bedroom and carefully got up on it. As she reached for the boxes on the top of the shelf, she felt the chair tip. She couldn't catch herself and knew she was going to hit the wood floor. She tried to brace herself and protect her belly. But she hit the edge of the dresser on the side and then the bed and then the floor. She knocked the breath out of herself.

Rosie came running when she heard the crash. "Mommy, Mommy, what happened? Why are you on the floor? Can you get up? What should I do, Mommy?" Rosie cried.

Nellie Mae finally managed a small smile and answered. "I'm alright, sweetie. Just let me catch my breath."

She laid quietly for a few moments and then thought she could get up by herself. She got to her knees and carefully used the side of the bed to get onto her feet. She felt alright. She was sore but she felt the baby move so she thought everything would be just fine. She walked slowly to the rocking chair and sat down. Rosie would not leave her side all afternoon.

After resting for a couple of hours, she needed to start making supper. She pulled herself up and started walking towards the kitchen. Suddenly she felt a sharp pain and something running down her upper thigh. She didn't want Rosie to be frightened so she said. "Rosie, Honey, I want you to go get our neighbor, Mrs. Nelson, quickly. Run as fast as you can, please."

Rosie ran out the door yelling for Mrs. Nelson to come help. Nellie Mae got herself into the bathroom. She was afraid she was losing the baby because she saw blood in her underwear. She grabbed a towel and laid down on the floor putting her feet up on the toilet seat.

By the time Mrs. Nelson arrived, Nellie Mae was certain she was having contractions and was having a miscarriage. She was devastated.

Mrs. Nelson rushed into the bathroom. "Oh Nellie Mae, what happened? I'll call Hank right away, dear. Try to stay calm and relax."

As soon as Hank arrived, he took Nellie Mae to the base hospital. The doctor examined Nellie Mae and told her that she was right, she had a miscarriage.

He wanted to keep her overnight to make sure she would not have any further bleeding. He told Hank that she had lost their baby.

Of course, Hank was heartbroken. "Will Nellie Mae have any lasting problems, doctor? Will she be able to get pregnant again, do you think?"

"I'm sure she will conceive again, Hank. She needs some rest and then she needs to get stronger and take it a little bit easy for a few weeks. But she is young and healthy. This just was an unfortunate accident." the doctor answered.

After an overnight stay, Nellie Mae felt strong enough to go home. She rested every day and tried to remain optimistic. It seemed like she couldn't get past the aches and pains. She just felt exhausted.

She was surprised that she wasn't losing weight or that the size of her belly hadn't gone down because she didn't feel like eating very much. She had not had a return of her monthly visit from Aunt Flo either.

She was a bit concerned about all the symptoms for several weeks. Hank kept asking her if she was feeling better. She told him she was fine but in her heart, she knew something wasn't quite right.

Finally she decided she should see the doctor again to find out what was going on. As she laid on the examination table and was explaining how she felt, the doctor was listening to her heart and taking her blood pressure and so on.

He palpitated her abdomen area. He got a surprised look on his face. He grabbed his stethoscope and put it on her belly. After a few minutes, he carefully pressed on various parts of her abdomen.

"Nellie Mae, have you felt anything in this area where I am pressing?" The doctor asked.

"Not really, I felt a few pops like I had gas from time to time but nothing painful. What is it, Doctor? What's wrong now?" Nellie Mae asked quickly.

"I don't think anything is wrong, Nellie Mae. I think there is an explanation for your symptoms." the doctor answered with a smile on his face. "In fact, I am sure I can already know what is the cause of the fatigue and no weight loss at this time. I think I hear a heartbeat going on inside. Let me see if the x-ray machine is available and we'll just see what is going on in there." the doctor said quickly.

"An x-ray? Is that necessary, Doctor? Is it safe if there is a baby inside me?" Nellie Mae asked anxiously.

"Yes, it's safe and it's necessary. Just wait here and I will get the machine and we will just see for ourselves." The doctor quickly exited the examination room.

He was soon back with the machine and another doctor. "This is my colleague, Nellie Mae. He's more expert in looking at x-rays so I thought it would be a good idea to have his opinion as well. Let us get this set up and we will take some films."

After the doctors had taken the films to another room to be developed and reviewed and they had discussed the results, they returned into the examination room and said they had some news for Nellie Mae.

"What is it? Is there something wrong with me? Please tell me right away, doctors." Nellie Mae begged.

"We have both agreed on the diagnosis and the films have proven our theory. You ARE still pregnant! It is possible that you were pregnant with twins and when you had the miscarriage, you lost one of the babies! So, you are definitely still pregnant and should be due just as I told you before which is about the first of November. I'm going to watch you carefully to make sure this baby is growing and safe. So, Congratulations, Nellie Mae. You will have wonderful news for your husband tonight."

It was indeed a wonderful evening for the little family. Hank was thrilled and Rosie started talking about a new baby again. Everyone vowed to make sure that Nellie Mae rested and took it easy.

"No more climbing on chairs or doing anything that could be dangerous to you or the baby, my darling." Hank said to Nellie Mae. "Promise me right now that you won't do anything that could harm either of you again."

"I promise. I do! I want this baby to be healthy and arrive safely too." Nellie Mae said.

The rest of the pregnancy went well. Nellie Mae got bigger every day or...so it seemed. She tried to stay off her feet as much as possible. She spent a lot of afternoons reading story books to Rosie to keep her daughter entertained.

The first of November cameand went. Nellie Mae was really tired of being pregnant. She felt awkward, fat, ugly and exhausted. She couldn't wait for the baby to be born. Soon it was almost the end of November with no signs of a birth soon

After a simple Thanksgiving meal, Nellie Mae went to bed early. She woke up just as dawn was breaking and felt some discomfort. She recognized the feelings and knew she must be in labor. She got dressed and woke up Hank.

When he realized it was time to take her to the base hospital, he went to the next door neighbor and asked if she would take Rosie. Of course, Mrs. Nelson was willing. Nellie Mae gathered some clothes for Rosie. She tucked Annie inside the blanket that Hank wrapped around the sleeping child. As soon as he came back, Nellie Mae was waiting by the door with her suitcase.

When they arrived at the base hospital, Nellie Mae was taken away to the maternity ward, which was just a screened off area. She quickly progressed into heavy labor and was ready to deliver. Hank was waiting out in the waiting room.

After what seems like hours, a nurse came out to talk to Hank. "Apparently the baby is a big one. Nellie Mae can't deliver in the normal way. Doctor has to perform a cesarean section. It may take a bit longer to get her prepped but everything should be just fine. I'll come back later and keep you advised on the progress." the nurse said.

Hank was really concerned now. A cesarean? Oh no! Hank bent his head and said a prayer or two that everything would go well. He knew this meant that Nellie Mae would have a longer recovery period. And how would he be able to take care of Rosie by himself?

After another hour, the nurse finally came out. She was smiling. "You have a big baby. Very healthy and very active. You have a son! He's got dark fuzz for hair and he has been putting up a fuss ever since he was born. Would you like to see him or your wife first, sir?" the nurse asked.

Hank had a big grin on his face. "Wonderful news! Please, I want to see my boy. I've waited a long time for a child. I must see him right now!" Hank answered quickly.

"Oh, I thought you already had a daughter! My mistake. You must be excited to have a baby boy. Please come this way, Captain Hamilton." the nurse said with a smile.

She led him to a small room that was the nursery. He saw his son. He was perfect in every way. Dark fuzz for hair and all his fingers and toes. He even opened his eyes for a moment before he started to cry. He must have had huge lungs because his cries were loud…very loud! Hank chuckled as he looked at his son. "How much does my boy weigh, nurse?"

The nurse looked at the chart. "He weighs 9 lbs. 3 ounces. Nellie Mae will have to stay in the hospital a few extra days because of the operation. The baby will stay here with her so she can nurse him."

"Now, are you ready to see your wife? She's very tired and the anesthetic is starting to wear off but I know she wants to see you. Please come this way. You can visit with her for about 15 minutes and then you must leave so she can rest. We will be taking the baby into her to try nursing after her nap."
The nurse took Hank to see Nellie Mae and left.

"Hello, my darling. Do you know how happy you have made me today? A son…a big handsome boy for me to take fishing and play ball with and teach all the things a father wants to teach his boy. I can't believe that I finally am a father with a child that is MINE!" Hank said to his wife.

"Oh, Hank. I can't believe what you just said to me. You are FINALLY a father? What about Rosie? You ARE her father too! Are you still feeling like she is a stepchild and that she isn't as important to you as our baby boy will be? I'm really sad that you said that just now. Please just go. I need to rest. I'll talk to you tomorrow." Nellie Mae slowly turned over onto her side and closed her eyes.

Hank realized that what he had said was wrong. He didn't mean to hurt Nellie Mae's feelings at all. But he had to confess that he did feel like the baby boy was his first child. He did care about Rosie but she wasn't really his. He would have to be more careful about what he said to Nellie Mae in the future.

He decided he needed to go home. He wanted to ask the neighbor if Rosie could stay at her house until Nellie Mae was able to come home. And he needed to get the baby cradle out. He wanted to give it another coat of varnish. He also needed to make sure all the baby clothes were ready for his son. There would be no pink outfits for his boy! He was very excited. He could hardly wait to talk to Nellie Mae about an appropriate name. What would sound good with the last name of Hamilton?

Hank discussed the situation with the neighbor. She was more than happy to keep Rosie. She said her children were enjoying playing with her and they all got along very well.

She also suggested that Hank come over to eat with them when she made supper every night That way he could spend time with Rosie before she had to go to bed. She told Hank that Rosie needed to feel like she was still loved with a new baby coming home in a few days. Rosie would need extra personal attention from both of her parents now. Hank hesitated and then agreed that it was a good idea.

He would tell Nellie Mae the next day. Maybe that would help smooth things over between them.

As the week flew by, Hank and Nellie Mae discussed baby boy names and talked about the new housing unit they would have after the first of the year. It should work out very well. By then, they hoped the baby would be sleeping all night.

It would be nice for Rosie to have her own room with room for all her toys too. Hank told Nellie Mae he had completed the doll cradle. He had decided to give it to Rosie when the baby and Nellie Mae came home from the hospital. Seeing the smile on Nellie Mae's face made Hank realize that had been a good idea that he had.

He was working on a doll house now. He was going to keep it a surprise for both Rosie and Nellie Mae. If he could get enough furniture made, it would be a Christmas gift. He thought Nellie Mae might be able to make some little curtains and blankets and a tiny table cloth out of scraps of fabric. And maybe they could find a little doll family to live in the house. That should show Nellie Mae that he was really trying to be a good father to Rosie.

Finally the big day arrived. Hank went to pick up Nellie Mae and his son. Before they could leave, however, they had to name the baby for the birth certificate. They discussed Edison for their friend and even Bernard in honor of Bernadette. They decided they wanted to put the past behind them so they finally selected the name of William Harold. He would be called Billy for a nickname.

When Hank got Nellie Mae and Billy home, he walked next door to get Rosie.

Mrs. Nelson asked Rosie to get her clothes and her doll while she talked to Hank. "I don't want to alarm you right now, Hank, but something unusual happened this week."

"I noticed a dark blue car with a Navy decal on the license plate driving on the base. I couldn't imagine why a Navy man would be here. I saw him driving slowly around the area. He seemed to be looking for something."

"In fact, when Rosie was outside playing with my boys, he stopped. He had red hair like hers and he called to her and tried to get her to come to the car. I went outside and called all the children over to me and sent them into the house. Then I asked the man what he thought he was doing? He just said he thought he recognized the daughter of a friend. Then he drove away."

Mrs. Nelson continued. "I talked to the neighbors and asked them to keep an eye out for the car or the man. I don't like the fact that he is driving around our little neighborhood when our children are outside. I'm probably being silly but I just had a funny feeling about the whole thing."

Rosie came running back into the room. "I have all my things, Papa. Can we go home now?"

"Of course, sweetie. Please thank Mrs. Nelson for allowing you to stay here this week."

Rosie quickly thanked Mrs. Nelson and gave her a hug.

"Let's go right now, Rosie." Hank said a quick thank you to Mrs. Nelson as he left without commenting on her news. That was the last thing Nellie Mae needed to hear about right now.

As he walked Rosie home, he explained that there was a surprise...well...actually two surprises for Rosie!

Rosie was so excited to have surprises that she skipped all the way home, holding Hank's hand. "Oh, Papa, I can't wait to see what the surprises are. Did you "bringed" me something special? I love you so much. And not just 'cause you "bringed" me a surprise but just because you are my Papa."

As they got to the house, Hank put his finger up to his lips and said. "We have to be very quiet when we go inside. I will show you the first surprise and then I will show you the biggest surprise of all. So, let's be very, very quiet."

Rosie giggled. "I'll walk on my tippy toes, Papa. I'll be really quiet too." she said in a whisper. Hank opened the door quietly and they went inside.

There on the floor was the doll cradle that Hank had made for Rosie. Next to it was the cradle for the new baby too.

"Oh, Papa!" Rosie said in a whisper. "It's a baby bed for my baby Annie, isn't it? It looks just like the cradle you made for me when I was a baby. Now the new baby can sleep in it too. It's so nice, Papa. Thank you." she said as she pulled on his arm and gave him a kiss on the cheek. "Can I play with it now?"

"Let me check to see if the other surprise is ready. Stay here and be as quiet as you can, Rosie." Hank said softly. He smiled at her joy in the little cradle he had made her. She really was a sweet little girl. He needed to remember how much she loved him as her Papa. It wasn't her fault that her real father was a stranger with red hair.

Hank peeked into the bedroom. Nellie Mae smiled and said softly. "Billy just nursed and he is asleep. Is Rosie here? I can't wait to see my favorite little girl. Please, Hank, bring her here."

Hank went out to get Rosie. He told her she had to stay quiet like a tiny mouse but she was going to see the surprise now. He led Rosie into the bedroom. When she saw Nellie Mae, she almost jumped on the bed but then she remembered she had to be quiet.

She tiptoed to the side of the bed. "Oh Mommy, I have missed you. You were gone for a very long time. I stayed with the neighbors. Was that alright?"

"I said please and thank you. I ate all my supper even the **va-get-tibles**...those icky green ones! But I ate them all and I helped dry the dishes too. But I'm really glad you are home now. Why are you in bed though? Is you sick?" Rosie said with a worried look on her face.

"Oh no, Honey. I'm not sick. I had to go to the hospital to get a surprise and it just made me very tired. I will be just fine. Do you want to see the surprise now?" Nellie Mae said. "Ask Papa to lift you up so you can see."

Hank lifted Rosie up and she looked at the tiny blue bundle in her mother's arms. "What's that, Mommy? Is that the surprise? I can't see what's inside the blanket. Is it a doll like Annie? I don't need another doll right now. Papa made me a doll cradle but I don't think two dolls will fit in it."

Just then, Billy made a noise and squirmed enough so that the blanket came open. Rosie's eyes got very big. "What's that, Mama?"

Nellie Mae smiled and said "Rosie, this is our new baby. He's your little brother. The baby is a boy. His name is William Harold but we are going to call him Billy. He is going to be noisy for a little while. When he is hungry or has a wet diaper, he may cry a bit. But he's going to be alright once he is fed. I will need your help to take care of him. Will you do that for me? I know you will be a big help and a very good big sister too. So what do you think?"

Then Nellie May said "Do you want to see all his fingers and his toes? He's very sweet. He can't do a lot of things yet because he is just a baby."

"Oh Mommy. He is very small. He's like a doll, isn't he? Yes, I want to help! I will bring you the diapers and the baby clothes and whatever you need. Can I hold him? I'll be "***berry***" careful really. Can I, please?" Rosie begged.

"Yes, you can hold him but only when Papa or I help you lift him. He can't hold his head up by himself yet. So we have to be gentle with him."

"Papa, will you put Rosie next to me and I will put Billy in her arms?" Nellie Mae asked.

"Sure, I can do that." Hank responded. "Here we go, Rosie. Sit next to Mommy and I will put a pillow on your lap so Billy can rest on it. Here he comes, Rosie, get ready to hold your baby brother." Hank said with a smile.

Nellie Mae put Billy in Rosie's arms. Rosie's eyes got very big. "Oh, Mommy! He's so sweet. I love him already. Can I give him a kiss? I'll be "***berry***" careful. Please?" Rosie asked.

"Of course, you can kiss him. Be careful of the top of his head. It's very soft so we don't want to bump it. But go ahead and kiss him. I know he will want you to love him." Nellie Mae said.

Rosie carefully gave Billy a very soft kiss on his cheek. "Oh Mommy, he smells so good! He smells like that powder you put on me sometimes. Did you put that powder on him too?" Rosie asked.

"Yes, I did. When he has a wet diaper, I clean him up and put a little powder on him and a clean diaper. When you see me change his diaper, he will look a little bit different down there than you do but that is because he is a boy. Boys and girls have different parts so we know whether they are a girl or a boy. Does that make sense, Rosie?" Nellie Mae asked.

"Sure does, Mommy! Mrs. Nelson next door had to change Tommy's diaper. He's bigger than Billy and he is starting to walk but he still wears diapers. I brought her the clean diaper and I saw him. He did look funny but Mrs. Nelson said that was because he was a boy and not a girl." Rosie said. "So, do you need a clean diaper for Billy yet? I can bring one if you do."

"Well, yes. You can bring me one. I"ll wait while Billy takes a little nap. But I will keep the clean diaper here so I have it ready. Thank you, Rosie. That is very helpful."

"Tomorrow I will get out of bed and I will need lots of help doing things around the house. I am so glad to have you here to help me get everything taken care of. You are such a good big sister already, aren't you?" Nellie Mae said with a smile.

"Now I think I need to take a nap too while Billy sleeps. Maybe Papa will get you a cookie and some milk while I am asleep. Later you can help Papa make scrambled eggs and toast for our supper tonight." Nellie Mae added.

"Scrambled eggs and toast? That's for breakfast, Mommy. We don't eat breakfast at night for supper!" Rosie said as she giggled.

"Well, tonight it will be a special treat. We can have bacon and eggs and toast and maybe cookies for dessert. How about that? A special party just because Billy is here." Nellie Mae said with a smile.

So Hank and Rosie left the bedroom. Rosie played with Annie and put her to bed in the new doll cradle. Hank checked the refrigerator to make sure they had bacon and eggs and bread. He knew he could manage that simple supper. Then it would be time for Rosie to have a bath and go to bed.

He was so happy to have his whole family home together. He thought about the past week and realized that he did love his life. He was a father to a newborn son...and a sweet little redheaded stepchild.

CHAPTER FORTY ONE ~

The supper was very good and everyone ate so much that they were just stuffed. Nellie Mae took Billy to the rocker by the fire and nursed him. Rosie was interested in what was going on.

When Nellie Mae asked Rosie if she had any questions to ask, Rosie said no. Rosie said that Mrs. Nelson had fed her son Tommy like that too. Mrs. Nelson told her that when mommies have children, they can make milk from their own bodies and feed them.

So Rosie was happy that her mommy could do that too. Rosie asked Nellie Mae if she had fed Rosie that way when Rosie was a baby. Nellie Mae assured her that she did. She told Rosie that because Rosie was such a good baby; it didn't hurt at all and it helped Nellie Mae learn how to do it very well.

Soon Rosie was yawning. Nellie Mae asked her if she was tired. "Oh no, Mommy. I want to stay up and help you with Billy. I can stay awake all night to help you."

Nellie Mae said "Well, maybe tonight I will just do it by myself because I am tired too. I want to go to sleep as soon as Billy is finished nursing."

"I have a good idea though. What if Papa puts some of my special bubbles in the tub tonight? You can have a warm bubble bath and then pick out your favorite night gown. And you can put Annie to bed in her new cradle too. When you are ready for bed, Papa will bring you into our bedroom and I will read you a story before Papa tucks you into bed." Nellie Mae said. "Now scoot, pick out your night gown while Papa gets the bubbles ready."

Rosie found her favorite pink night gown and Hank had the tub all ready for her. He helped her into the tub and watched her play with the bubbles for a few minutes. Rosie was getting very sleepy so Hank lifted her out, dried her off and helped her get into the night gown. He carried her into their bedroom and held her while Nellie Mae gave her a kiss.

She was so sleepy that Hank said he would put her into bed and read to her until she fell asleep. He had only read about two pages of her book when he looked to see her eyes were closed and she was already sound asleep. He smiled at how sweet she looked and thought again about what a good girl she always was. She really was very special.

Then he walked back into his bedroom and saw that Nellie Mae and baby Billy were also asleep. He picked up Billy and took him out to the living room to rock. He talked softly to Billy and told him all about the plans he had. He would teach Billy everything he knew. How to fight if necessary. How to climb trees. How to fish. How to play baseball. How to camp out and hike. He was really looking forward to the days when Billy was old enough to do those things. But in the meantime, Hank vowed to protect his son from anything that could harm him. He carried Billy into the bedroom and put him in the cradle near the bed.

Then he started thinking again about what Mrs. Nelson had told him. It sounded like the red headed man was not going to give up easily. Hank realized he would have to tell Nellie Mae very soon about the news. She would need to know that Mrs. Nelson was suspicious of the man already. And Nellie Mae would have to be very careful about Rosie being outside alone.

CHAPTER FORTY TWO ~

The next day Rosie was up early and eager to help Mommy with the baby. She loved bringing a clean diaper and helping to give him a bath. Mommy had reminded Rosie again that boy babies look a little different than girls.

Rosie smiled and said "Mommy, I know that. Mrs. Nelson had to change her little boy and she told me that boys and girls look different so we can tell them apart."

Nellie Mae smiled to herself. Well, at least she didn't have to explain anymore than that fact right now. There would be plenty of talking when Rosie got old enough to understand. Nellie Mae also told Rosie that she had to nurse Baby Billy many times a day so he would grow up big and strong and smart like Rosie.

After Billy was ready for a nap, Nellie Mae asked Rosie to watch over him in his cradle while Mommy took a bath and got dressed. Nellie Mae quickly took a bath and came back into the bedroom. There was Rosie singing a song to Billy while she gently rocked the handmade cradle. "What a beautiful sight" thought Nellie Mae. "My little family is perfect, a girl and a baby boy , what more could I ask for?"

Later in the day, Nellie Mae started a quick and simple supper of soup and sandwiches on home baked bread. The kitchen smelled delicious. Rosie could hardly wait for Papa to come home. She put the dishes carefully on the table and carried the glasses one at a time. "Mommy, can I pour the milk too?" Rosie asked.

"Better let me do that this time, sweetie. The milk jug is full and it's very heavy. But it won't be long before you will be strong enough to do it for me. You can put some spoons on the table for the soup, though. That will be a big help to me. And what should we have for dessert? Mrs. Nelson brought over a peach pie today. Shall we have it tonight?" Nellie Mae asked.

"Oh yes, Mommy!" Rosie answered. "Papa loves peach pie. So that will be a special surprise, won't it?"

Soon Hank came home. As soon as he walked through the door, he went straight to the cradle to see Billy. He carefully picked him up and brought him out to the kitchen.

"Look at our little man, Honey. Isn't he sweet? I love how he smells. I can't wait until he is old enough to do things with. I have all kinds of plans for us when he is bigger. And how was your day, my darling?" Hank asked. "Did everything go well for you?"

Nellie Mae gave him a long look. "My day was just fine, thank you. Rosie was a big help to me. She brought me clean diapers and watched Billy while I took a bath and got dressed. She set the table and checked on Billy all afternoon. Don't you want to say something to your daughter?"

Hank glanced at Rosie. "Oh, of course. I'm sorry, Rosie. I should have said Hello to you too. It sounds like you were very helpful with Billy today. Thank you for helping Mommy."

Rosie ran over to Hank and gave him a big hug. "I missed you today, Papa. Even when I was busy helping Mommy take care of Billy.

She tried to climb into his lap but he was holding Billy. "No, Rosie. I have Billy in my arms. I can't hold both of you right now. Maybe later." Hank said.

Nellie Mae said "Hank, put Billy back in the cradle or lay him on a blanket by the fireplace. It's time to eat and you don't need to be holding the baby right now. He's sleeping."

Hank reluctantly put Billy on a blanket near the fireplace. He walked quietly to the kitchen and sat in his chair. As they bowed their heads to pray, Rosie asked if she could say the blessing.

"Of course, sweetie. Go right ahead." Nellie Mae told her daughter.

"Dear God. Thank you for the soup and stuff. I want to thank you for Baby Billy too. I love him already. And thank you for Mommy and for Papa. He's the best Papa ever. Amen." . Rosie said with a smile on her face. "Ok, let's eat!"

Later that evening when the children were settled in their beds, Hank brought Nellie Mae a cup of her favorite tea. As they sat together on the couch in front of the fire, they talked quietly about the children and other neighborhood subjects.

Finally, Hank turned to Nellie Mae and took her hand. "Honey, there is something else I must tell you now. I didn't want to worry you but I must let you know what has been happening. The day I brought you and Billy home from the hospital, I went to get Rosie at Mrs. Nelson's house, remember?"

"Of course I remember, Hank. So did Rosie misbehave or something? Was Mrs. Nelson upset with Rosie? I can't imagine that Rosie would do anything naughty. She loves to play with the Nelson children." Nellie Mae said quickly.

"No, no, darling. It wasn't anything like that." Hank said. "No..., what Mrs. Nelson said to me was that while you were in the hospital, she saw something. She saw a dark blue car with a Navy decal driving around the neighborhood. She said all the children were playing in the front yard, including Rosie. The man stopped the car and called to Rosie trying to get her to come to him. He had red hair too."

"Mrs. Nelson went right outside and shooed the children into her house. Then she asked the man what he was doing. He told her he thought he recognized the daughter of a friend. When Mrs. Nelson tried to question him further, he drove away!"

Nellie Mae had a frightened look on her face. "Oh no, Hank! Do you think it was Bernie's brother-in-law? Is he trying to find out if there was a baby after all? What are we going to do now, Hank?"

Hank patted Nellie Mae's hand. "Try not to worry, honey. We will just have to be more watchful. Maybe we should remind Rosie not to talk to strangers or go near any cars that she doesn't recognize. For now, at least, that should keep her safe. Besides, I imagine she will want to be inside the house helping you with Billy. She does seem to love him very much, doesn't she?"

"Yes, she does. That's a good idea. I don't want to scare her but she does need to remember about being safe, especially with people she doesn't know. I'll talk to her tomorrow morning." Nellie Mae said. "So, now let's go to bed, I'm exhausted and Billy will be up again soon, I'm sure of it."

CHAPTER FORTY THREE ~

Life settled into a routine in no time. Baby Billy got on a schedule and Nellie Mae and Rosie had plenty of time to spend together. Rosie continued to be a wonderful big sister. She loved to watch Billy's every move. She reported to Mommy every time Billy did anything whether it was to yawn or stretch.

One day, Rosie ran into the kitchen. "Mommy, Mommy, guess what Billy just did? Guess!" she said excitedly.

"What, sweetie. What did he do now?" Nellie Mae answered.

"Well, he tried to roll over! He almost did it too. I was going to help him but I thought it would be better for him to learn how to do it. Does he need help, Mommy?" Rosie asked.

"No, you did the right thing. He is getting stronger and now he is going to try new things. That's very exciting. Maybe you can tell Papa when he gets home tonight." Nellie Mae said.

"Now, I need to start supper. How does beef stew sound with homemade biscuits?"

"Mmmm, that sounds so good. Can I help cut up the potatoes after you peel them? I'll be very careful with the knife, Mommy." Rosie asked.

"We'll see, Rosie. I have some carrots and green beans to put in the stew too. Maybe you can help me measure the ingredients for the biscuits and mix them for me. And…maybe you can use a cup to cut out the biscuits if you would like to do that. That way you can tell Papa that YOU made the biscuits." Nellie Mae told her daughter.

"Oh boy! I can hardly wait." Rosie laughed. "Won't Papa be surprised at what a good helper I am? So, what should I do first? Oh, I know, I need to wash my hands really good with soap and then I need an apron like you wear, right?"

"That's right, Rosie. Here's an apron. I think this one will fit you. I'll tell you how much flour and salt and milk to use and then you can mix it up. But first I need to start the stew. So, do you want to wash and then snap the beans for me? I'm certainly glad I have such a good helper today." Nellie Mae said with a smile.

As they prepared the dinner, they talked about the neighborhood and the other children Rosie played with and what they should fix for supper the next night.

Nellie Mae asked Rosie if she had seen any new cars driving around lately. But Rosie said she hadn't, so Nellie Mae just reminded her about not talking to strangers and changed the subject.

Rosie continued to help Nellie Mae every day in the kitchen. Nellie Mae decided to make a little apron to match one of hers for Rosie. Maybe she could ask Hank to build a little kitchen for Rosie to play with. She would save some of the cardboard boxes of cereal and some food containers too to be pretendfood. Nellie Mae recalled that she had always enjoyed pretending to be a mother and take care of her pretend family. It seemed like Rosie was going to follow in her mother's footsteps for sure. But at least Rosie would know how to cook and do housework before she got married!

When Hank arrived home, he could smell the stew bubbling on the stove. Nellie Mae was taking a pan of hot biscuits out of the oven. They looked a bit odd and misshapen but they smelled great.

Nellie Mae told Hank that Rosie had made the biscuits herself. Rosie asked her Papa to have the first one. Hank hesitantly took one and put some butter on it. As he ate it, he looked surprised.

"Oh, Rosie. I think this is the best biscuit I ever had. It's even better than Mommy's! Could I please have another one?" Hank asked.

"Sure, Papa. I made a bunch of them. You can eat as many as you want. Can't he, Mommy?"

Nellie Mae smiled at her husband. Now that was the way to treat his daughter. Hank smiled back at Nellie Mae and gave her a wink.

After the supper dishes were done with Rosie's help, Nellie Mae asked Hank to fill the bathtub with her special bubble bath again. She went into Rosie's bedroom and picked out a clean night gown for her daughter.

"Aren't you going to get into the tub while the water is hot, darling?" Hank asked her.

"No, Hank. The bubble bath is for Rosie. She worked very hard today helping me. I'm giving her a special treat before she goes to bed."

"Rosie, sweetie, come into the bathroom. Papa fixed you a bubble bath to thank you for the good biscuits and all the help you gave me today."

Hank took Rosie into the bathroom where he helped her jump into the tub. She played with the bubbles until they were almost gone. Then she put on her clean night gown and came out to the living room to say goodnight. As Nellie Mae started to get up to tuck her into bed, she asked Rosie what story she wanted to hear tonight.

"Would it be all right with you, Mommy, if Papa reads me a story tonight?" Rosie questioned.

"Why, of course it would. Papa? Rosie would like you to read her a story and tuck her into bed. Isn't that nice?" Nellie Mae gave her husband a look.

He reluctantly put the newspaper down and got up. Rosie grabbed his hand and pulled him into her bedroom. She picked out a story book and crawled into bed.

"Sit by me in the bed, Papa." Rosie said. "I picked out my favorite story about the handsome prince and the princess. I think you are more handsome than this prince though."

Hank started reading the story. As he read, Rosie snuggled next to him and soon she was falling asleep. As she started to close her eyes, she murmured "Papa, I love you so much. I'm glad you tucked me into bed tonight and read me a story. I liked the bubble bath too. It smelled so.good..." Rosie was asleep.

Hank carefully got up and placed the blanket around Rosie's shoulders. He turned off the light and walked quietly out of the room

"Is she asleep already, Hank?" Nellie Mae asked. She was nursing Billy by the fire and had a quilt tucked around both of them. "She is such a sweet child. I'm glad you are trying harder to treat her like your daughter. She really loves you so much."

Hank smiled. "Yes, she almost fell asleep before I had read the first five pages of the storybook. I guess that warm bath relaxed her. She is a lovely little girl. I'm trying to get past my old feelings when they pop up. I know I should be so grateful to have such a lovely daughter. I do want to be a good father to her."

Hank sighed. "And I have to admit that it is getting easier to forget that she isn't really my child." Hank glanced at Nellie Mae and saw her eyes get angry. He quickly changed the subject and asked her what she was going to do the next day.

Hank realized he needed to keep his mouth shut about his feelings for Rosie. Nellie Mae was not having any of it and it always caused stress between them.

CHAPTER FORTY FOUR ~

As soon as the holidays were over, the family was able to move into their new larger housing. Luckily it was just around the corner from their old place so Mrs. Nelson was always available if Nellie Mae needed a sitter in a hurry.

Nellie Mae was very busy getting settled in. Billy was sleeping through the night. Rosie loved having a bigger bedroom. Hank had made a tiny kitchen for Rosie for Christmas. She had it all set up in her bedroom and spent hours playing there with Billy. Billy scooted and rolled around the room and took her toys off the lower shelves. Rosie didn't mind as she patiently put the toys back in place.

Rosie also tried to do as much as she could to help her mommy. Working along side Nellie Mae in the kitchen became a special time for both of them. She loved the little apron Nellie Mae had made her. Nellie Mae also gave Rosie some child sized kitchen utensils to use as her very own. Rosie felt like a big girl even though she was just over 3 years old.

One evening Hank came into the house and seemed unsettled. He didn't talk too much during supper. While Nellie Mae and Rosie were doing the dishes, Hank walked down to the base's woodshop to work on some new projects. He was trying to make a china cabinet for Nellie Mae. It would be an anniversary gift. As he started into the woodshop, his neighbor, Tim Nelson, approached him.

"Say, Hank! I'm glad I ran into you. My wife said there used to be a dark blue car that drove around the base. The driver was a red headed man, right?" Tim asked Hank.

"The reason I ask is that a man stopped his car and asked me if I knew of any little girls with red hair around the base. I thought he might be looking for Rosie. I asked if he had a name and he didn't. But he said her last name might be Dawson. There"s no Dawson family around here that I know of. I told him I didn't know of any Dawsons and he left."

"When I mentioned the conversation to my wife, she told me that someone who had red hair had been here before. She thought he might be referring to Rosie too but she didn't tell the man anything. So what's the story? Is he a relative or something?"

"Did you say the car a dark blue one?" Hank asked. "The man has been asking around before. I don't know why he is obsessed with finding a red headed little girl. It's not Rosie. But I don't want him to know where Rosie lives in case he is just a bad person. I'm afraid he might do something to her."

"I'm going to ask the Base Commander why this man has been able to get past the guards at the front gate so many times. Thanks for the heads up, Tim. But please keep this information discrete so other people don't talk to him, will you?"

"Of course! No problem. If you need any more help with it, just let me know. A couple of my good buddies are with the base police division. I can tell them to keep an eye out too if you want." Tim responded.

"That would be a good idea. Thanks again, Tim." Hank answered. As Hank walked into the woodshop, he vowed to keep an eye out for the dark blue car. He would have to talk to Nellie Mae. Maybe they should remind Rosie again not to talk to any redheaded man or go near any people she doesn't know on the base. He didn't want to scare Rosie but he didn't want the man to question her either.

When Hank returned home that night, he told Nellie Mae the news. She was frightened. He assured her that he was going to the Base Commander and get the guards at the front gate on the alert too. He also suggested that they have a conversation with Rosie the next morning. When she was outside, she was always playing with the other children. Much of the time she had Billy with her so if they told her that the man might do something to Billy, they knew she would never let that happen.

In checking with the guards at the front gate and the Base Commander, Hank learned that the man had a military ID and that was why he was allowed inside the base. The Commander told the guards not to let the man inside any longer. Hank didn't tell the Commander the real reason he was worried. He just told him that he believed the man had stalked his family at their previous base before they had been reassigned to this base and he was concerned.

CHAPTER FORTY FIVE ~

Everything was quiet after that. Hank started to relax and feel like he had done all he could to protect his little family. He was working on spending more time with Rosie. In fact, he suggested to Nellie Mae that they each take turns putting the two children to bed each evening. It was a good plan and Rosie really enjoyed having her Papa all to herself every other night. Hank also enjoyed getting to know her even better. He looked forward to her chatter when he got home. He made time to talk to her about her day as soon as he got home. Then while she was in the kitchen with Nellie Mae, he had plenty of one-on-one time with Billy too.

Hank continued to work on the china cabinet for Nellie Mae's anniversary surprise. He had located some beautiful maple and cherry wood. He wanted to incorporate the pieces into the doors of the cabinet along with glass inserts. It was very detailed work and he spent many hours laying it out and rearranging the wood pieces.

One evening he was working on a specific area and had to make some delicate cuts. He was using a band saw. He thought about changing the blade because it seemed a bit dull but he was in a hurry and didn't want to take the time.

It was almost supper time so he quickly turned on the saw and started making the cut. As he worked, the blade got caught in a piece of wood and got stuck. Without thinking, he gave the wood a hard push with his right hand. His thumb and palm went into the moving blade. There was blood everywhere.

Hank just looked at his hand in puzzlement. Why couldn't he feel his hand? Then he saw the blood and realized he had cut himself very badly. He tried to get to the door to call for help. But everything went dark before he could reach the door.

At home, Nellie Mae was waiting for Hank to come home for supper. She turned down the chicken and covered the mashed potatoes. She looked outside and could see the light was on in the woodshop. She waited a few more minutes and then called to Rosie.

"Honey, put on your coat and go get Papa. He must have lost track of the time. Hurry now and be careful. Watch for cars or strangers too. And remember what we told you a few weeks ago." Nellie Mae instructed.

"I will, Mommy. I look all around when I am outside now just like you told me. I'll get Papa and we will be right home. It's his turn to tuck me into bed tonight and I already have picked out a story book for him to read to me." Rosie quickly put on her coat and went out.

As Rosie walked to the woodshop, she could hear the saw running. She thought Papa was probably very busy working on the surprise for Mommy. Papa had told her all about the big surprise and she was proud that she didn't tell Mommy by accident. At least, not yet!

She went to the door and looked in. She didn't see Papa at all. All the lights were on and the saw was running. As she opened the door, she saw a lot of red stuff all over the floor. She looked down and saw Papa lying down.

"Papa! Papa! What's the matter with you? Wake up. Are you sick? Did you fall down? Are you hurt?...Papa?" Rosie tried to shake Papa and wake him up.

"Ooooh, what? Where am I? Who is talking to me?" Hank muttered.

"It's me, Papa. It's Rosie. Can't you open your eyes? Wake up, Papa. Are you going to be all right? Please wake up, Papa. You're scaring me. What's all this sticky red stuff all over. Did you spill some paint?" Rosie said with a whimper.

"Oh, Rosie. Thank goodness, it's you. Can you run to Mrs. Nelson for me and see if her husband is home? Please hurry, honey. I need some help to get up. Can you get me a clean rag from the pile on the table? And don't touch the saw, baby." Hank said.

Rosie answered "Yes, I'll get Mr. Nelson for you. Here's my coat to keep you warm while I am gone. And then I will tell Mommy that you need help."

As Rosie started out the door, she saw a flash of headlights turning the corner. She stopped and looked. It looked like that dark blue car that Papa and Mommy had talked about. She hid behind a trash barrel until the car turned the corner. Then she quickly ran across the street. She saw the headlights again at the next corner. She could see the driver's face and he had red hair!

She was very frightened because Papa had said the man was bad and might be trying to take Billy away. She climbed over the fence into a back yard and crawled across the grass to the next fence. As she started to climb that fence, she saw the car again. She ducked down and waited until the car had moved past her. She climbed that fence and finally got to the Nelsons house. She went to the back door and knocked.

Mrs. Nelson opened the door. "Quick! Turn off the light please, Mrs. Nelson! That car with the man with red hair is driving around. I'm not supposed to let him see me." Rosie whispered.

"What, dear? What are you talking about? Rosie, where is your coat? Why aren't you at home having supper with your family? Just what is going on here?" Mrs. Nelson asked her.

"Mrs. Nelson, can I come inside? I'm cold. And is Mr. Nelson home? Papa is hurt at the woodshop and he told me to ask Mr. Nelson to come help him. There's sticky red stuff all over him and the saw is still running. I covered Papa with my coat because he was shivering and he told me to come here right away. Can Mr. Nelson go help Papa?" Rosie said.

"Oh my! Come inside, Rosie. Tim, Tim, come right away! Rosie said that Hank is hurt at the woodshop and he sent her here to get help. Go quickly!" Mrs. Nelson said.

Tim Nelson rushed out the front door and ran to the woodshop. He checked on Hank who was unconscious in a pool of blood. Tim tried to bind up his right hand in clean rags to stop the blood that was flowing so quickly. Then he ran to the infirmary for help.

As soon as Tim had left, Mrs. Nelson turned to Rosie and said "Ok, Rosie. Here's what we are going to do now. I am going to lock all the doors while I go tell your mother what has happened. I want you to stay here with my children. They are already in bed so you must be quiet. Don't leave the house. Don't answer the door if anyone knocks. I have a key and can let myself back in. Try not to be afraid, Rosie. You have done such a good job so far." Mrs. Nelson gave Rosie a hug and left by the back door.

After Mrs. Nelson told Nellie Mae what was going on, Mrs. Nelson suggested that she take Billy back to her house for the night. Nellie Mae quickly gathered up clean clothes for her children and put on her coat.

"But I don't understand, Mabel. Why didn't Rosie come here first?" Nellie Mae said. "I know she wanted to get Tim to help but why didn't she come home after that then?"

"She said she saw the dark blue car and the red headed man driving. She hid and then climbed all the backyard fences to get to my back door. She was afraid that he would see where she lived if she came here. She's safe at my house with all the doors locked. I told her not to leave. I'll take Billy home through the back yard and lock us all inside my house. Hurry now and get to the infirmary to check on Hank, dear." Mabel responded.

Mrs. Nelson carried Billy and a bundle of clothing and diapers back to her home. She unlocked the back door and called out to Rosie. "Rosie, it's safe now. I have Billy. I talked to your mommy and she wants you and Billy to stay with me all night."

"She will come get you in the morning. Let me fix you some soup to eat. You must be very hungry and very tired. I have your doll, Annie too so you can sleep with her tonight on the couch. Come along to the kitchen now, dear."

Rosie could barely hold her head up long enough to eat the hot soup. She was exhausted. She laid down on the couch and fell asleep before she could change into her night gown. Mabel tucked Annie into Rosie's arms and pulled a quilt up over her. Mabel settled into a chair with Billy and tried to sleep too.

Mabel was very concerned that the red headed man had shown up once again. Just who was he and what did he want? Why was he looking for a red headed little girl on this base?

And why in the world would he think Rosie was that little red headed girl anyway? Anyone could tell she looked just like Nellie Mae except for the red hair. Mabel made a note to ask Nellie Mae who had red hair in her family.

CHAPTER FORTY SIX ~

At the infirmary, the doctor worked quickly to repair the damage. Hank had lost a lot of blood. Tim offered to give a transfusion because he knew he was the same blood type. After that blood transfusion was completed, Tim decided to go home to his own family. By then, Nellie Mae had arrived at the infirmary to sit with Hank.

The doctor told Nellie Mae that it was a miracle that he saved Hank. "If it wasn't for the fact that your daughter covered Hank with her coat, he could have gone into shock. She did a good job. She probably helped to save his life. Hank should be fine. I reattached the tendon and sutured the wounds. He is going to be very sore tomorrow. It will take a few days for his strength to return. But I think he will have full function of the thumb and the hand. If you like, you can see him now and stay with him too."

Nellie Mae went into the cubicle. Hank was turned on his side away from the door opening. Nellie Mae approached the bed and touched his shoulder.

"Hank, Hank, my darling. Are you awake? Can you talk to me?" Nellie Mae asked.

Hank rolled over and groaned. "I'm awake. My hand is hurting. The doctor told me to keep it up on this pillow to try to keep the swelling down. I don't know what happened or how I got here. I can't remember a thing. Do you know?"

"I most certainly do, Hank. Apparently you cut your hand on the band saw in the woodshop. I had sent Rosie down to get you because you were late for supper. She put her coat on you to keep you warm and then she ran to Mr. and Mrs. Nelson's house to get Tim to come help you." Nellie Mae said.

Hank's eyes got very big. "Rosie did that? Rosie,..our little girl was able to do all that by herself?"

Nellie Mae answered " Yes, Hank. Rosie! She was so brave because when she was leaving the woodshop to get help, she saw that man. That man in the dark blue car. She even saw his red hair. She hid behind a barrel until he passed by. Then she climbed a backyard fence. Well, three fences actually until she got to the Nelsons back yard. She knocked on the Nelsons kitchen door and told them what had happened to you."

"The doctor just told me that she probably helped save your life because she put her coat on you before she left you in the shop.. The doctor said you could have gone into shock. She did that and she's not even 4.years old, Hank. NOT EVEN FOUR YEARS OLD YET!"

Hank looked at Nellie Mae. "Oh my, what a brave and smart little girl. But where is she now? Is she safe? And what about Billy?"

"They are both at the Nelsons for the night. Tim just went home. He was going to contact the guards at the front gate and ask why the man got inside the base again."

"Hopefully they can find him if he is still here and put a stop to this nonsense. I'm tired of living in fear. He is not going to take my daughter and I will NOT live in fear for the rest of my life either." Nellie Mae said angrily.

Hank took her hand. "No, we are not going to live like this any longer, Honey. I promise you that. Tomorrow I will get some answers and we will get this resolved once and for all, my darling."

Nellie Mae gave Hank a kiss and then she crawled into his cot and they went to sleep in each others arms.

CHAPTER FORTY SEVEN ~

When Hank was released from the camp infirmary, he went straight to the guards at the front gate. He told them that Rosie has seen the dark blue car with a redheaded man as the driver.

He asked to see the check-in list for the previous night. When he checked it over, he saw the last name of Dawson. So the man must be Ed's brother from the Navy. He questioned the guards about the man who had been inside the base. What was his reason for being there and why was he allowed inside?

The guards said they had just be reassigned to the front gate and hadn't seen the restriction on the list. They told him they were now aware of the situation and would not allow the man back inside again. If necessary, they would call the base police to escort the man away. They apologized to Hank over and over. He told them the man had been stalking his family. He did not want the man to have any access to his family members.

Then Hank went to the Base Commander. Hank advised him that Rosie had been frightened when she saw the dark blue car with the red headed driver. He also told the Commander that he had already spoken with the front gate guards and they were well aware of the situation.

When Hank got home, he relayed all the information to Nellie Mae. Nellie Mae asked Hank "Do you think that the man is Bernie's brother-in-law then? What should we do if he starts talking about his sister-in-law's baby to our neighbors?"

Hank replied "Well, first of all neither Bernie nor Ed ever lived on this base so no one will know the names. Secondly, if his name was never on the birth certificate for Rosie, how could he prove he was involved with her conception? And how would he know that YOU actually gave birth to Rosie anyway? I don't think we need to worry now."

"I don't know. I don't have a good feeling about this, Hank." Nellie Mae said with a sad smile. "I just don't feel safe here anymore. Is there anything else we can do?"

Nellie Mae added "What if he talks to Bernie's parents and tells them his story? If we show up with a redheaded daughter who could be about the age he would claim the baby would have been by now... how are we going to explain it?"

Hank shook his head. "Now, don't be getting yourself all upset. I don't really think we will have any more problems with Ed's brother. If he knows both Ed and Bernie have passed away, he could just assume that the baby passed away too since Bernie would still have been pregnant when she took her own life." Hank told Nellie Mae. "Honey, try not to think about it too much. I'll keep checking with the base police and the front gate guards too."

Nellie Mae signed and then she said. "I'll try not to worry too much. I can do that. I'll keep my eyes open any way but I know you will take care of any problems that come up for your family. I do feel much better now that you are home with us again too."

CHAPTER FORTY EIGHT ~

The weeks went by very quickly as Hank continued to recuperate. His hand got better and he had almost full function of his thumb. With the help of Tim Nelson, he did finish the handcrafted china cabinet for Nellie Mae. He gave it to her for their anniversary. Nellie Mae was so proud of it. She enjoyed seeing her better dishes on display through the glass windows. It was a very special gift indeed.

The weather was starting to warm again. The children loved playing outside in their back yard. Sometimes they also played with the neighbor children. There were no more sightings of the dark blue car or the red headed man either. Hank and Nellie Mae were breathing a sigh of relief. They no longer checked the streets every time they went outside. Nellie Mae still made Rosie and Billy play in the back yard as much as possible so she could see them. And the back yard gate was kept locked at all times too.

Hank had asked the Base Commander if he would check with the Navy about any red headed men with the last name of Dawson. Hank wanted to find out where the man was stationed or if he was still in the Navy.

The Commander told him a few days later that a man who had used the name of Thomas Dawson was still in the Navy and had recently signed up for another tour. He was currently on leave. The only address they had for him was back in Minnesota where his parents were living. Hank hoped that if Thomas was Ed's brother that he had given up any thoughts of finding the red headed child he had been searching for.

About three weeks after that, Nellie Mae got a letter from Ed's parents that had been forwarded by the Chaplain from the previous base. They did still live in Minnesota and were wondering if Nellie Mae had any information about Bernie that she could share.

The letter said that Ed's brother, Tom, was sure that Bernie had been pregnant. They wondered what had happened to the expected baby. Did it pass away when Bernie took her own life after learning that Ed was killed in the war? The parents were begging Nellie Mae to ease their minds and tell them what had happened.

Nellie Mae was torn. How should she explain it? She thought the best thing was to tell them that the baby was miscarried. They might have known that if Tom said he had seen Bernie or written to her.

But, of course, Tom would know what he did to try to give Bernie another baby so he might still think there had been another baby on the way. What if Bernie had kept in touch with Tom? What if she told Tom there was a pregnancy? Oh my, what a big mess this was turning into. Nellie Mae decided she would ask Hank what to do when he got back home.

Nellie Mae prepared a good supper that night and waited for Hank's arrival. After dinner and after Rosie had taken her bath and both children were tucked into bed for the night, Nellie Mae and Hank settled at the kitchen table for some tea and more dessert.

Nellie Mae said "Hank. I got a letter today from Ed's parents asking again about the baby that Bernie was carrying. They are questioning what happened to it."

"I was going to say that Bernie had a miscarriage and never told anyone but me about it. I was also going to say that she was very depressed and when she learned of Ed's passing; she just couldn't go on."

Hank answered "That sounds like a good idea, Nellie Mae. It would make sense that if she lost the baby and then learned that Ed was killed that she would be so despondent that she took her own life."

"But, Hank, there's still a problem." Nellie Mae said. "Ed's brother, Tom, knew that he came to get her pregnant. Well, he thought it was her. And what if Bernie wrote to him and told him she was pregnant? Would it be a better idea to tell Ed's parents she lost that baby too?"

Hank shrugged his shoulders. "But how would Tom explain to his parents that he was involved in trying to get her pregnant? Wouldn't that seem odd to them? Wouldn't they want to know why? Even if he told them Bernie had a miscarriage and wanted another child for Ed, isn't it a far stretch for Tom to say that he was involved? I don't think he would admit that to his parents. Do you, Nellie Mae? It just seems so wrong to upset his parents like that."

"That's true, Hank. That's a very good point. But what if the parents were so anxious to have a part of Ed that they didn"t care if Tom was the reason for a baby? I'm still very worried about what to say to them." Nellie Mae answered.

"I think you should just say that she lost the baby and was very depressed as a result. You tried to encourage her to tell her parents and Ed's parents at the time but she was afraid that the news would get back to Ed overseas. And that when she got the telegram about Ed being killed in action, that she just went into a bigger depression and took her life. Even if she was pregnant by Tom, it would seem logical that the baby died when she did." Hank responded.

"I guess you are right, Hank." Nellie Mae. "'I'll write the letter tomorrow and send it on its way."

Hank smiled at Nellie Mae. "That's for the best, I think, my darling. Now are you ready for bed and a good night's sleep?"

CHAPTER FORTY NINE ~

Nellie Mae did write the letter. She had a few photographs of Bernie so she decided to send them along too. She would take the bus to town and go to the main Post Office. She asked Mrs. Nelson if she would watch Billy for her since he still needed an afternoon nap. Mrs. Nelson agreed and gave Nellie Mae some letters of her own to mail.

Nellie Mae told Rosie that they were going on an adventure and would be taking the bus. Of course, Rosie had to get Annie, her doll, ready to go. She put Annie in her best little doll dress and then wrapped Annie in a blanket. Then Rosie put on her own sweater. She was waiting by the door as soon as Nellie Mae came out of her bedroom.

"I'm all ready, Mommy." Rosie said as she giggled. "I can't wait to ride the bus. Can I put the coins in for the fare this time?"

"Of course you can, Rosie. I have some mail to take along. We will be going to the big Post Office in town. And if we still have time, maybe we can stop at F.W, Woolworth's Five & Dime to look at fabric for a new dress for you." Nellie Mae answered.

So off they went, mother and daughter, on their little trip to town. They walked to the post office and got the mail sent out for Mrs. Nelson and the small package with the photos and the letter for Ed's parents. Nellie Mae felt a sense of relief once the package was in the hands of the US Mail. She hoped the photos and her information would do the job and that Ed's parents would be satisfied.

Nellie Mae and Rosie walked a few blocks to look at the spring fabric at Woolworth's. They found several adorable patterns and had a hard time picking just one of them. There were so many pretty fabrics that would be perfect for Rosie's new dress.

But finally Rosie chose the one with little pink and red rose buds. Rosie told her mother that it was perfect because her name was Rosie so she should have a rose patterned dress. Nellie Mae thought she might even have enough scraps to make a matching doll dress for Annie. Wouldn't Rosie be surprised!

They caught the bus to go home and made it there in time to fix a meat loaf and baked potatoes for their supper before Hank got home that night. After the children were tucked into bed for the night, Nellie Mae told Hank about her day.

"I really feel so much better now that the letter and photos have been mailed out." she said. "I hope it helps Ed's family accept that the baby is gone just as Bernie is. I don't want them to be hanging on the hope that there is still a child waiting to be found."

"I hope so too, Nellie Mae. I know you didn't want to lie but this is the best way to handle it, I think." Hank responded.

As Hank drank his last cup of tea, he wondered about the red headed man ~ Ed's brother. Was he gone for good by now or was he going to show up again trying to get onto the base.

CHAPTER FIFTY ~

Nellie Mae didn't hear anything more from Ed's parents. She hoped that she could put all her fears behind her now. She didn't want to have to hide her feelings from her children. Sometimes Rosie asked Nellie Mae if she was sad because Rosie said that Nellie Mae was very quiet. Nellie Mae told Rosie that she was thinking about many grown-up things.

Nellie Mae decided that she should start sewing that little pink and red rosebud fabric into a very adorable Easter dress to keep her mind off the other situation.

She got out the fabric and pinned the pattern to it. She cut out the pieces and decided to start working on it. Maybe she could get enough of it done so that Rosie could try it on for size tonight. She sat in her favorite rocking chair by the window and began to sew.

Suddenly the door burst open. It was Rosie. "Mommy, Mommy! I saw the dark blue car again. The red headed man was driving it! Is he coming to get Billy? Can we take Billy to Mrs. Nelson's so the man can't find him? I'm afraid, Mommy, I'm so afraid." "Rosie said as she burst into tears.

"It will be alright, Rosie. I will take Billy to Mrs. Nelson's right now. I will lock our doors. You stay away from the window and wait for me to come back. I don't know how that man got inside the base again. But don't worry, baby. I will take care of it." Nellie Mae said.

She grabbed some clothes and Billy and ran next store. She told Mrs. Nelson that the red headed man had been spotted by Rosie just a few minutes before. She asked Mrs. Nelson to keep an eye out for him. Nellie Mae then ran back to her own home and pulled the curtains and locked the door.

She peeked out and saw the dark blue car come down the street. It drove slowly past her house and continued on. She let out a sigh of relief. After a few minutes, she looked out the window again.

Then she heard a knock at her back door. She quickly went to the door to see who was there. As she peeked out, the red headed man was standing there. She shut the curtain and ducked down onto the floor. Rosie saw her and her face went white. Nellie Mae put her finger to her lips to stay quiet as Nellie Mae crawled across the kitchen floor to Rosie's side.

Nellie Mae whispered to Rosie. "Go into your bedroom and shut the door, Rosie. Don't come out for any reason until you hear my voice or Papa's at your door. Get under your bed and stay as quiet as a tiny mouse. Don't be afraid, baby. It's going to be alright. I promise you." Nellie Mae told Rosie. "Now scoot as fast as you can, sweetie."

The man knocked at the back door again. He called out Nellie Mae's name. "Nellie Mae, Mrs. Hamilton? I'm Tom Dawson. Ed was my brother. I know you live here because you sent a letter to my parents. I just want to talk to you for a few minutes, please. I just need to ask a few more questions."

"I'm not here to harm you. I just need some answers. Please open the door, Mrs. Hamilton. I know Bernie was your best friend. If she confided in anyone, it would have been you."

Nellie Mae thought for a moment. If she opened the door and talked to Tom, she might be able to convince him that there is no child. She might be able to stop this once and for all. She thought about the pros and cons and decided she should open the door.

"Just a minute, I need to get dressed first. Give me a few moments to do that and then I will open the door for you." Nellie Mae answered Tom.

Nellie Mae checked to be sure Rosie had closed her bedroom door. She quickly picked up Annie and threw the doll into the china cabinet. She looked around the room to see if there were any other signs of a little girl. Then she walked back into the kitchen and peeked out the back door.

Tom was standing there. He looked very much like Ed had looked except his hair was red. Red just like Rosie's hair.

Nellie Mae unlocked the kitchen door and opened it. "I don't know what else I can tell you. I wrote a detailed letter to your parents. Apparently they got that letter? I...uh, I sent photos too. Did they like the photos? I thought they might enjoy seeing some that I took when Bernie was...um...when she was still pregnant right after Ed went overseas that first year. I hope the photos didn't upset them too much." Nellie Mae said, wringing her hands.

"Yes, they got the letter and the photos. And yes, they were happy to get both. But I...um...I had some questions of my own. I had talked to Bernie after she had the original miscarriage. She was very upset and didn't want to tell anyone. She did tell me that she had confided in you. She even said you had been very helpful to her during that time." Tom said.

"Did you know that I had visited Bernie for a couple of weeks before I shipped out, Nellie Mae? May I call you Nellie Mae?" Tom asked. "Yes, I was at her old base for about 10 to 12 days. I was trying to help Bernie. And then she wrote to me a few times while I was overseas. Did she ever tell you that, Nellie Mae? Did she confide in you at all?"

"Um, well, no. She didn't tell me you visited her. I am surprised because we spent every day together and sometimes we had supper together too. So, when were you visiting? How long ago?" Nellie Mae asked Tom. She was having a hard time looking into his eyes. She was sure she was turning red because she was lying to him.

"I was with her just over 4 years ago. And she wrote me for a few months. She said she was pregnant and was expected to deliver around Thanksgiving that year. She said the pregnancy was going very well and she was very excited about the baby. But then, she got the news about Ed's death. And then we heard that Bernie had died too. I was just wondering what happened to that pregnancy? Did she have the baby early? Or did she lose the baby when she died? I can't believe she would take her own life when she was going to have that baby she had wanted so much in just a few more months." Tom responded.

"Oh, uh, well, um…I...I don't know, Tom." Nellie Mae stuttered. "I don't know what happened. She didn't have the baby early. I do know that! So she must have lost it. That's really sad because she was looking forward to the baby coming. I never thought about what happened to the baby. I guess I just assumed it passed away when she did. I'm sorry for your family's loss, of course."

Nellie Mae watched Tom. His eyes started to have a mean look. His face turned red.

"I think you DO know what happened to that baby, Nellie Mae! I think you stole that baby away from Bernie and that is why she took those pills. I think you know exactly where that baby is...well, actually the kid would be close to 4 years old now. I've heard there is a redheaded little girl on this base. And I think I have seen her. So what can you tell me about that, Nellie Mae? What did you do with the child? It belonged to Bernie and Ed so now it belongs to my parents and me. We want that child. She belongs to us. So where is she? Where in the hell is she?" Tom demanded.

As he approached Nellie Mae, she started to back up into the living room. She didn't know where to go. Rosie was still in the house and she didn't want Rosie to come out of her bedroom. Tom might take her away.

"You're wrong, Tom!" Nellie Mae said. "I do have children. Two children but they belong to my husband, Hank and to me. I didn't steal Bernie's baby, I didn't! Please believe me, Tom. You should leave. My husband, Hank, will be home soon and he won't be pleased that you are here in our home. Please go!"

"I'm not going anywhere until I see your children for myself. I will just wait until Hank gets home if necessary. I don't have anything to lose. I don't have any family except my parents and they don't even know I am here. I think you are lying to me to cover up the fact that you stole Bernie's baby. So let's see those two brats you have. Bring them out here so I can see them. And don't do anything foolish either, Nellie Mae."

"Ok, Ok. I have to go get them at the neighbor's house. They were playing with her children this afternoon. So you can wait here and I will be right back. You don't have to worry, I will come right back." Nellie Mae pleaded.

"Make it fast. I don't want to stay here any longer than I have to. So don't try anything stupid. Get your butt over to the neighbors and get right back here. I will be watching out the window to see you too." Tom said angrily.

"Ok, it will take me a few minutes to get them. The baby is probably asleep and I will have to get all his things, his bottles and his diapers and so on. But I will be back as soon as I can be. I promise, Tom." Nellie Mae said quickly.

She ran around the corner and pounded on the door. When Mrs. Nelson opened the door, Nellie Mae quickly said "The red headed man is inside my house, Rosie is hiding in her bedroom. I told him that I had two children over here and he demanded that I bring them back with me. Can I take your son, Charlie to pretend to be my son too? Please, Mabel, I need your help. And can you get in touch with the base police or with Tim to find Hank? Please, I'm begging you." Nellie Mae cried.

"Charlie, come quickly! Go with Mrs. Hamilton and don't say a word. There's someone in her house that she is afraid of. I have to get your father or Mr. Harrison as fast as I can. Go quickly now." Mrs. Nelson said to Charlie.

"But Mom, I can run faster and find Dad or Mr. Hamilton. Why not send Timmy Jr. He doesn't talk much anyway so he won't tell anything to the man, right?" Charlie said quickly. "I'll go out the back door when Mrs. Harrison leaves from the front. I'll run as fast as I can too."

Mrs. Nelson nodded. "That's a great idea, Charlie. Ok let's get Timmy Jr. and Billy ready to go. Help me, Nellie Mae, so we can get this done."

Soon Nellie Mae was carrying Billy and his extra clothes and holding onto Timmy Jr.'s hand. Timmy Jr. didn't look anything like her so she hoped the switch would work and that Tom would fall for it. As she opened her front door, she almost passed out.

There was Rosie, sitting on the couch crying. Tom was standing over her with a big scowl on his face. "Oh, so you finally came home? And just who are these two little boys? Decoys? What do you have to say for yourself, Nellie Mae?"

"I, um..well, I'm holding Billy, he's my son and this is Timmy. He's the neighbor's little boy. Mrs. Nelson and I trade babysitting sometimes so I brought him here."

"Rosie, Sweetie, are you alright? Why did you come out of the bedroom? Did this man do anything to you? Answer me, Rosie, please, Honey." .Nellie Mae begged her daughter.

She dropped Timmy Jr.'s hand and put Billy on the floor behind her. She went to Rosie and grabbed her into her arms. "Tell me that you are OK, Honey, please."

"She's fine. I didn't do anything to her. I just checked the bedrooms while you were gone and found her hiding in the closet. So I brought her out here."

"I have to say she is a beautiful child. Just about the right age too. And her hair is the same shade as mine. Isn't THAT interesting?" Tom said. "So what do you have to say for yourself, Nellie Mae? How did you wind up with my child?"

"Your child?" Rosie said. "No, mister you're wrong about that. Mommy and Papa have told me the story about when I was "borned "many times. They drove to the hospital in a Jeep. It was very cold and I was "borned" there in the hospital. Then they brought me home and we moved. So I can't be your child, mister ."

"I think your red hair is nice and it does look like mine but you can't be my Papa. I have a Papa already and a Mommy too...and a little brother. His name is Billy and he's right there playing on the rug."

Tom stood there with his hands on his hips and started to laugh. "So, I can't be your Papa, eh? Well, we'll see about that. I imagine a blood test could help with that, right, Nellie Mae? What do you think we should do about this strange turn of events? Shall we go to the base infirmary and check our blood types? I have an unusual type so if Rosie does as well that should help me prove I am her father."

"No, you are not taking my child anywhere, Tom. You can wait until Hank gets home and talk to him. Now if you will excuse me, I need to start supper. You can stay, of course. Rosie, please go wash your hands and start peeling potatoes for me." Nellie Mae said.

"But, Mommy, you never let me use the ...Oh, sure I will, Mommy. I'll go start peeling right now. But what about Timmy Jr.? Should someone take him home? Should I do that first, Mommy?" Rosie said quickly.

"No, you are not going anywhere, Rosie." Tom said. "You can go into the kitchen and help your mother with supper but you are staying here. I think Timmy would like to stay for supper too, wouldn't he, Nellie Mae?" Tom said with a smirk.

"Oh, of course, Timmy can stay. He can play with Billy while Rosie and I get supper started. So, how are you doing on those potatoes, sweetie?" Nellie Mae said as she walked toward the kitchen.

She whispered to Rosie "See if you can get to the kitchen door and sneak out to the neighbors. Be as quiet as you can. I'll be fine with Tom. I don't think he will hurt anyone now. I"m going to put some alcohol in his coffee and try to make him sleepy too. Let me try to distract him and then you run."
.
"Oh, Tom, do you want some coffee? I can make some fresh for you. I haven't had any since breakfast and I like to have a fresh cup while I am cooking!" Nellie Mae called out to Tom. She quickly put the coffee into the percolator and set it on the stove.

"Sure, Nellie Mae. That sounds real good about now. It will help me stay awake too since I have been up all night driving to get here."

"Do you want to know how I found you? When you sent the package to my parents, you put on your return address on the package. Not too smart of you, Nellie Mae, was it?" Tom said with a laugh. " You brought me right here. Right here to my redheaded little girl. How about that?"
Nellie Mae needed to get to the whiskey so she moved towards the cupboard and lifted the bottle out. She wanted to add as much of it as she could to his cup. But when she started to pour it, Tom walked into the kitchen.

"Where's Rosie at?" he barked. "Where is that little redheaded brat anyway?"

Rosie came around the corner where the pantry was next to the back door. "Oh, I'm right here. I was looking for a big pot to put the potatoes in." Rosie said.

Rosie went on "Oh, mister? Do you like biscuits?. I make very good biscuits or so my Papa says. Doesn't he, Mommy? So how about some biscuits with dinner tonight? They don't take too long to make." Rosie said with a little smile.

"Sure, kiddo. That sounds great. You are going to be a big help to your grandma when I take you home to her. Won't she be surprised at how well you can cook too!" Tom laughed.

"What did you say?" Rosie said quickly. "Oh no, you must be mistaken. I can't leave my mommy and Papa and Billy to help someone else. I have plenty of work to do here helping Mommy take care of Billy and Papa. Why would you think I would want to go with you anyway? I don't understand."

Nellie Mae quickly walked in-between Rosie and Tom. "Um, Rosie, I need some more flour for the chicken. Would you get that new box in the pantry? Take a bowl and pour some in it. It's the box with the red drawing on the front. Go see if you can find it for me, will you? Just be careful not to spill it on yourself. And then be sure to wash your hands good with soap before you start the biscuits."

"And, Tom, the coffee is ready. Would you like anything in it? Sugar, milk, or both?" Nellie Mae said to Tom.

She was trying to distract him so Rosie could try to get out of the house. "I can bring you a cup if you want to sit in the living room. The couch is quite comfortable."

Rosie was puzzled. Was she supposed to try to get out the kitchen door or was she supposed to look for some box in the pantry? She looked at Nellie Mae and tried to figure out what the plan was.

Nellie Mae started walking into the living room with the coffee cup. She nodded to Rosie and looked toward the door. Rosie understood that she was to try to leave. She slowly and quietly walked toward the door and started to reach for the door knob. But Tom called her name.

"Rosie, come here. I want to talk to you now about my plans. It will be a bit of a drive to get back to my parents' house so we will need to leave very soon. Go pack your clothes and decide what you want to take with you. Once we get going, I am not ever coming back here again." Tom said with a frown on his face. "So get in your room and get your junk packed."

Rosie looked desperately at Nellie Mae. What should she do?

Nellie Mae nodded "Yes, Rosie , go ahead and pack. You can put your things in a pillow case. Don't forget Mabel. You will want to take your dolly friend to talk to."

Rosie was confused. Take Mabel? What was Mommy talking about? Oh, wait, I bet she is trying to tell me to go out my window and run to Mrs. Nelson's house for help. That must be the plan.

CHAPTER FIFTY ONE ~

Rosie quickly went into her room and started to shut the door as much as she could. She opened her closet door and started pulling hangers with clothes out of the closet. She banged around and then wound up her little jewelry box that played a tune. She pushed her kitchen set up to the door to try to block it off.   She thought maybe she could get out of her bedroom window and run to Mrs. Nelson's. If she could barricade the door enough so that Tom couldn't get inside her bedroom quickly.

She called out to Nellie Mae. "Mommy, should I take my winter coat too? And my skates and my underwear?"

"Yes, of course, sweetie. Take everything you want to have with you. I think you left Mabel in the china cabinet last night when you were pretending to send her on a trip."

Nellie Mae tried to bang some pots around to make more noise too. She got a big skillet out to start heating up the grease to fry the chicken. As she was working, she had an idea of how she might be able to distract Tom.

"Rosie, can you come get Billy and wash his hands for me. Supper will not be ready for about an hour but I'm sure his face and hands need washing with soap. Take Timmy with you too, honey." Nellie Mae said as she turned up the flame under the iron skillet.

"Um, what, Mommy?" Rosie called out. "I didn't hear what you said just now."

Tom yelled "Rosie, open up your ears! Your mother said to come get these two brats and wash their faces and hands. Hurry up with it. We will have to be leaving very soon."

Rosie climbed over the kitchen set she had pushed in front of her bedroom door and managed to squeeze through the door. She came into the living room and got the boys.

She took them into the bathroom and ran the water in the tub. She whispered to them that they were going to play a game of hide and seek.

She locked the bathroom door and quietly opened the window. She told both boys to be very, very quiet. She lifted each boy and placed him out of the window. Then she climbed out too. She put her finger up to her mouth, picked up Billy and motioned for Timmy to crawl in the grass to the gate. It was locked! So she lifted each of them up and helped them get over the fence. She climbed up after the boys and dropped onto the grass behind her house. She picked up Billy again and ran with Timmy to Mrs. Nelson's backyard. Then she and knocked at the kitchen door.

Mrs. Nelson opened up the door and looked surprised. She whispered to Rosie. "What's going on at your house? Is your mother alright? Is that man still in your house, Rosie?"

Rosie whispered back. "Yes, he is. He wants to take me away with him to his parents' house. He made me pack my clothes. Mommy is trying to figure out how to stop him. I don't know what she is going to do. I'm scared, Mrs. Nelson. I'm really, really scared. Have you been able to find Mr. Nelson or my Papa yet?"

Mrs. Nelson responded. "I sent Charlie out to find them. He hasn't come back yet so I don't know where any of them are right now. I don't want to leave your mother alone with that man in her house. What can I do to help?"

"Well, I told the man that I could make biscuits and Mommy said to take a bowl into the pantry and pour something out of a box with red writing on it. I don't know what that would be, do you, Mrs. Nelson?" Rosie said.

"Oh yes, I do. It's rat poison. We all sprinkle it around the house in the autumn to keep the mice out. It will make anyone very sick if they eat it. She must be wanting to make it look like flour and hoping he will eat it. I have some in the pantry. So I could mix it up with something and take it over to your house. Do you think that might work, Rosie?"

"I don't know but I guess it can't hurt to try. I was supposed to be washing the boys faces and hands and I locked the bathroom door so that might make it harder for him to realize we are not inside." Rosie said.

"Alright then, I am going to mix up something quickly. Hmm. I have mashed potatoes already made. I can mix some in there and then add some to the gravy I made. That would be quick. And maybe put some in my homemade jam for the biscuits? Let me get to work." Mrs. Nelson said.

She flew around the kitchen mixing some rat poison powder into various pots and then put them in bowls and covered them over.

"Rosie can you crawl back over the fence and get back into your bathroom? I can walk over and knock at the front door while you are coming out of the bathroom. It should be a distraction for a few moments." Mrs. Nelson said.

"What about Billy and Timmy , Mrs. Nelson? Can we leave them here?" Rosie asked.

"Sure, let's take them into a bedroom and lock them in with some cookies and toys. Hopefully we won't be gone very long." Mrs. Nelson said.

Just then her older son walked into the house.

"Charlie, did you find your father and Hank? Nellie Mae is in terrible trouble at her house and I need to find a way to help her." Mrs. Nelson asked her son. She started putting the dishes into a box to carry.

"Yes, Ma. I did find both of them. They are getting the base police together and coming as soon as they can. So how about I take over what you were going to take to Mrs. Hamiltons house. Maybe I can help too." Charlie said.

"Yes, that's a great idea. This food has rat poison powder in it that will make the man sick. Don't let Nellie Mae eat any of it. Tell her it is my special recipe. Go quickly now. Rosie is going to sneak back into the house so the man doesn't know she was gone. Keep your eyes open and don't leave Nellie Mae and Rosie alone with that man."

Rosie went out the back door, climbed over the fence and ran to the bathroom window. Just as she was getting inside the bathroom, she heard Tom banging on the door. "What's taking so long in there, Rosie? Open the door." he demanded.

"Just a minute. I was just getting the boys out of the tub. They were so dirty that it seemed easier to give them a bath. Let me drain the tub and then I will be right out as soon as they use the toilet."

Rosie said in a loud voice "Oh, boys, time to get out of the tub. Let me dry you both off. Stop wiggling, you two! Ok, that's good. I'll help you get dressed and then you can come to the kitchen table for supper." Rosie said as she pulled the plug. She hoped Tom would fall for the lies. She unlocked the door and carefully opened it.

Just as she was leaving the bathroom, she heard a knock at the front door. "I'll get the door, Mommy." Rosie called out. She ran to the door and opened it. "Oh hello, Charlie. Come in. What do you have there?" she asked.

Charlie answered. " Hi Rosie! Mom made some extra potatoes and thought maybe you could use them with your dinner tonight. There's gravy too. And something for dessert. It might be vanilla pudding, I'm not sure. And she even parted with her homemade jam too. Anyway, she told me to give it to your mother and tell her it's a special recipe. Is your mother here, Rosie?" Charlie said.

As he walked into the living room, he saw the red headed man sitting on the couch. "Oh Hello. I'm sorry, Rosie, I didn't know you had company I'd better just carry this food into the kitchen and go back home."

"Mrs. Hamilton?" Danny called out. "Mom asked me to bring over some potatoes and gravy. She made too much for us and thought you might like to try her special recipe." Danny looked directly into Nellie Mae's eyes.

He whispered "Don't eat any of it. It's got rat poison powder in it. Do you want me to stay?"

Nellie Mae smiled. "Oh, Charlie. How nice of your mother. Would you like to stay for dinner too? I guess this is the day we all overcooked. I making fried chicken for supper. I never did get enough of our potatoes peeled so what you brought will be a good addition to the meal. I do have cornbread muffins though. I seem to remember that cornbread is one of your favorites?"

"Oh yes, I love them." Danny answered. "Sure, I'd like to stay. Ma doesn't make cornbread often so this will be a real treat."

Tom walked into the kitchen. "What's the hold up on the food? I can smell it and I'm sure it is good."

"But I'm in a bit of a hurry, you know, Nellie Mae. Let's get the food on the table so I can take Rosie and leave." Tom demanded.

"It's all ready right now, Tom." Nellie Mae said. "I'll just dish it up and we can sit down and eat."

Nellie Mae turned her back to Tom and put a huge portion of Mrs. Nelson' special recipe potatoes and gravy on the plate along with some chicken legs with more gravy poured on top. Then she buttered some of the cornbread and put Mrs. Nelson's jelly on the pieces she added to Tom's plate. She carefully put chicken and her own potatoes on Charlie and Rosie's plate and on her own.

She told Tom to sit down and eat while she checked on the little boys. Charlie and Rosie sat down and slowly started to eat from their own plates.

When Nellie Mae returned to the kitchen, she gave a little laugh and said the little boys had fallen asleep so she had covered them up. "I'll give them their supper when they wake up later. More potatoes and gravy, Tom?" Nellie Mae asked.

"Sure, this is really good, Nellie Mae. The potatoes have a special taste to them. Wonder what Mrs. Nelson's secret is? Do you know, Charlie?" Tom asked.

"Uh, no. I don't know much about cooking, sir. I like to eat though. Love this chicken, Mrs. Hamilton. And the cornbread is so good. I don't even need jam on it because it is so sweet." Danny added. "Could I have another cornbread please."

Tom said "That's a great idea. Give me two more pieces of the cornbread and put plenty of that jam on them. It's great! And if you've got any chicken left, I'll take some more of that too."

Nellie Mae refilled Tom's plate and handed Charlie the plate of cornbread. Rosie and Nellie Mae were very quiet and ate slowly. Nellie Mae wondered how long it would take before the rat poison powder started to work on Tom. If he would just get sick enough, maybe they could probably overpower him.

Just then Charlie said. "Boy, I wonder when my dad will be home?. He was looking forward to supper tonight because Ma was making his favorite. Beef and gravy over mashed potatoes. I guess that why she made so much of the potatoes and gravy by accident. When Dad knows his favorite meal is for supper, he makes a point to get home early."

Charlie stared at Nellie Mae to get her attention. He was trying to tell her that help was on its way.

Tom patted his stomach. "Oh, I think I actually ate too much for supper. I'm feeling a bit uncomfortable right now. Guess my eyes were bigger than my stomach after all."

"Oooh boy, my stomach is gurgling now! Hope it settled down soon so we can get on our way. Are you all packed, Rosie? We have to leave soon." Tom barked at Rosie.

Rosie looked up and smiled. "Yes, I am. I'll go get my stuff and put it next to the front door so we can go whenever you are ready. I want to brush my teeth first though. I'll be right back to help you with clearing the table and doing the dishes, Mommy."

Nellie Mae started to get up. "More coffee, Tom?" she asked. "There's still some left and it's hot. Might help to settle your stomach too."

"Sure, why not, Nellie Mae." Tom answered. "Give me a cup of it."

Nellie Mae poured the cup and then turned back to the stove. She put the coffee back on the burner and turned it on. Then she started to run water for the dishes. She was trying to keep Tom distracted.

Rosie came back too. She started to put the chicken away on a plate in the ice box. She asked Nellie Mae if she should save the potatoes and gravy. Nellie Mae shook her head. "No, sweetie, I'll just make fresh when your Papa gets home. The cornbread can be saved though. "Give me the potato and gravy and I will throw them into the garbage so I can wash the dishes."

As they started to clean off the table and put dishes into the soapy water, Charlie asked if Nellie Mae wanted him to empty the water tray under the ice box. "I do it at home for Ma every night. So I would be glad to help, Mrs. Hamilton."

Nellie Mae looked at Charlie oddly. Then she realized he wanted to distract Tom too. She nodded yes to Charlie and thanked him. Charlie pulled out the heavy water pan and carefully carried it to the back door. He poured the water outside and came back into the kitchen.

Tom was still sitting at the table. He didn't look very good. " Are you alright, sir?" Charlie asked him. "You don't look very good right now."

"I don't feel very well either, boy." Tom snapped. "How about helping me to the bathroom and I'll see if I can get some relief there."

Charlie assisted Tom out of his chair and walked him to the bathroom. When Charlie returned, he said. "Ok, we need to do something to get some control. I was thinking I could hit him over the head with the water pan. Or can you think of anything else, Mrs. Hamilton? We need to figure out something in a hurry too."

Just then they heard the sound of the toilet flushing. The door opened and they could hear footsteps coming down the hallway. Tom was groaning and belching all the way back into the kitchen.

"Quick, Charlie, there's some extra clothesline in the pantry on the top shelf. Get it and maybe we can tie Tom up. And yes, if you have to hit him on the head, do it." Nellie Mae said quietly.

Tom returned to the kitchen. "Is anyone else feeling sick?" he asked. "I can't believe how bad I feel. I don't think I ate anything that the rest of you didn't eat. I know I probably ate too much but I don't know why I...oh my...oh!" Tom grabbed a chair and sat down. "I feel terrible. Charlie, help me to the couch, will you?"

Charlie answered "Sure, I will, sir. Just let me put this water pan back first." Charlie walked behind Tom and hit him in the head. Tom started to get up but then sat down hard and his head hit the table.

"Quickly , Quickly, tie him to the chair with the clothesline, Charlie Oh hurry, please!" Nellie Mae cried.

"I've got him hog-tied, Mrs. Hamilton." Charlie said with a big smile. "He won't be getting out of that very soon."

Rosie turned towards her mother. "Mommy, if he comes to and starts any trouble, I'm going to hit him with the iron skillet. I don't want to do it but I won't let him take me away from you."

Just then there was a quick knock at the front door. Charlie went to open it with Rosie and Nellie Mae right behind him. There were some of the base police. "Oh good, you're just in time. We have the man tied up in the kitchen. Right this way."

As they all walked towards the kitchen, they had a surprise. Tom was untied and had a knife in his hands.

"You really didn't think I fell for that trick, did you, boy?" Tom grunted. "I've been in combat, kid. I know how to play like I am unconscious and then get myself out of bad situations. So, now what are all of you going to do? I'm taking Rosie with me and none of you are going to stop me."

"You men get back into the living room and sit on the couch. Rosie, get over here right now. I'm going to have to tie everyone up and then you and I will be on our way, got it?"

Rosie began to cry. "Yes, I know. I…I…could I go get my pillowcase of stuff and my doll, please? And don't hurt anyone. I'll go with you."

"Yeah, OK, but make it quick." Tom snapped. "And don't try anything either."

Rosie quickly walked out of the room to her bedroom. She grabbed her pillowcase and Annie, the doll, and ran back to the kitchen. She hugged Charlie and then went towards Nellie Mae.

"Mommy, I love you so much!" Then Rosie hugged her and quickly whispered. "Give me a big hug and then walk towards Tom."

Nellie Mae did as Rosie asked. She went toward Tom and asked if he wanted to take any food with him on the trip back to his parents. She started towards the refrigerator to keep his eyes on her.

"Come on, Tom. I know you will be hungry later and so will Rosie. So let me pack up the rest of the chicken and cornbread for you. It wont take but a minute." Nellie Mae said.

Tom sat down at the kitchen table again.. "Hurry up. I want to get out of here. And don't try anything stupid, either."

As he looked at Nellie Mae, Rosie quickly picked up her pillowcase and walked behind Tom. She pretended to bump into his chair and dropped her doll, Annie, in his lap.

"Oh, sorry. I'll get her." Rosie said as she swung the pillow case as hard as she could towards Tom.. She hit Tom in the head and he crumbled to the floor.

Then Nellie Mae ran over and hit him in the head again with the iron skillet. Tom was very still on the floor. Charlie and the men rushed him and got him tied up once again.

"Wow, Rosie! That was brave. What did you hit him with to make him pass out?" Charlie said.

"I guess it must have been my roller skates inside the pillow case. I just wanted to get him off balance so Mommy would have time to do something. I think it worked, didn't it, Mommy?"

CHAPTER FIFTY TWO ~

A few moments later, Hank and Tim arrived at the house. They helped the base police get Tom into custody. The base police told the family that Tom would be charged with attempted kidnapping and putting minor children at risk. They assured everyone that he would be put away for a very long time.

Nellie Mae was so relieved. Mrs. Nelson brought Billy back home and told Nellie Mae what was in the special recipes. Nellie Mae told everyone how helpful Charlie had been. And then they turned to Rosie.

"My sweet, sweet daughter. How did you do it all?" Hank asked Rosie. "I can't believe how brave you were. You protected our whole family, almost by yourself. You are so special to me. I don't think I can ever forget what you have done. You've been the best daughter any man could ask for, my darling child."

Rosie said "It was easy, Papa. I thought about what you would do and I did it. I tried to be just like you. I love my family…all my family so much that I would do anything to stay with all of you forever and ever and ever.

CHAPTER FIFTY THREE ~

After a investigation of Tom and his actions, he was charged with trespassing on a military base as well as the other charges and brought to trial in the military court. He was sentenced and placed into a military prison and was mandated to never contact Rosie and her family again.

Tom's parents had accepted Nellie Mae's explanation of what happened to Bernie and the baby she had carried. They attributed Tom's obsession with a baby to his need to help his family cope with the death of Ed and of Bernie. And even though they thought that Rosie looked a lot like Tom and Ed, they decided to just leave things as they were and move on.

Nellie Mae was thrilled to finally be able to go back to her home town and introduce her two children to her parents and her siblings. She told them she had been pregnant when Hank first left for overseas but didn't realize it right away. She also said with dealing with Bernie's miscarriage and Ed's death followed by Bernie's suicide that she just didn't feel up to communicating with her family right away. They vowed to stay in touch and to see each other much more often in the future.

Bernie's parents had no idea that Rosie's father was really Ed's brother who had red hair so they didn't question anything. Hank and Nellie Mae asked them to be the children's godparents which made Bernie's parents very happy.

Tim and Mabel Nelson never knew the complete truth about the mystery surrounding a redheaded little girl and a redheaded man. They decided that it was really none of their business and they kept their questions to themselves.

Rosie sometimes wondered about why the red headed man wanted to take her away. She thought he must be very sad and lonely, especially now that he was in prison. But she decided to just enjoy her family and continue to do her very best to be a good big sister.

And it was going to be very important to continue to help because Mommy had just told her another secret. Mommy was going to have another baby very soon. Rosie didn't care if the new baby was another boy or a girl; she was just happy to be the big sister.

And Hank? Hank realized that he had the best daughter he could ever have imagined. And now that he knew how lucky he was, he wasn't ever going to have any doubts about his love for Rosie.

And he never did.